DEBRIEFING THE PRESIDENT

www.**penguin**.co.uk

DEBRIEFING THE PRESIDENT

The Interrogation of Saddam Hussein

————

John Nixon

BANTAM PRESS

LONDON • TORONTO • SYDNEY • AUCKLAND • JOHANNESBURG

TRANSWORLD PUBLISHERS
61–63 Uxbridge Road, London W5 5SA
www.penguin.co.uk

Transworld is part of the Penguin Random House group of companies
whose addresses can be found at global.penguinrandomhouse.com

Penguin
Random House
UK

First published in Great Britain in 2016 by Bantam Press,
an imprint of Transworld Publishers

Published by arrangement with Blue Rider Press, an imprint of Penguin Publishing Group,
a division of Penguin Random House LLC

Book design by Amanda Dewey

Every effort has been made to obtain the necessary permissions with
reference to copyright material, both illustrative and quoted. We apologize
for any omissions in this respect and will be pleased to make the
appropriate acknowledgements in any future edition.

This does not constitute an official release of CIA information.
All statements of fact, opinion, or analysis expressed are those of the author and do not
reflect the official positions or views of the Central Intelligence Agency (CIA) or any
other U.S. Government agency. Nothing in the contents should be construed as asserting
or implying U.S. Government authentication of information or CIA endorsement of the
author's views. This material has been reviewed solely for classification.

A CIP catalogue record for this book
is available from the British Library.

ISBNs
9780593077788 (hb)
9780593077771 (tpb)

Typeset in 11.5/17pt Adobe Caslon Pro
Printed and bound by Clays Ltd, Bungay, Suffolk

Penguin Random House is committed to a sustainable
future for our business, our readers and our planet. This book
is made from Forest Stewardship Council® certified paper.

MIX
Paper from
responsible sources
FSC
www.fsc.org   FSC® C018179

1 3 5 7 9 10 8 6 4 2

For my mother, Helen, and my father, Richard

More is thy due than more than all can pay.

—*Macbeth*, act 1, scene 4

Contents

As required of all current and former employees of the Central Intelligence Agency, I submitted the manuscript of this book to the CIA's Publication Review Board. The PRB is charged with ensuring that neither confidential nor classified information is inadvertently revealed. *Debriefing the President* twice underwent extensive PRB reviews. The result is twofold: the manuscript's publication, unfortunately, was significantly delayed, and, throughout this book, you will find black bars used to indicate where the CIA's redactions were applied. I apologize in advance for any inconvenience, and regret that the CIA has censored some material that in no way compromises official secrets.

John Nixon

Prologue

Unfinished Business

But the participant has at least one vital contribution to make to
the writing of history: He will *know* which one of the myriad of
possible considerations in fact influenced the decisions in which he
was involved; he will be aware of which documents reflect the reality
as he perceived it; he will be able to recall what views were taken
seriously, which were rejected, and the reasoning behind the choices
made . . . If done with detachment, a participant's memoir may help
future historians judge how things really appeared, even (and perhaps
especially) when in the fullness of time more evidence becomes
available about all dimensions of the events.

—Henry Kissinger, *White House Years,* 1979

The rise of Islamic extremism in Iraq, chiefly under the rubric
of ISIS (or Islamic State in Iraq and al-Sham), is a catastro-
phe that the United States needn't have faced had it been willing
to live with an aging and disengaged Saddam Hussein. I do
not wish to imply that Saddam was innocent of the charges that
were thrown at him over the years. He was a ruthless dictator
who, at times, made decisions that plunged his region into chaos
and bloodshed. However, in hindsight, the thought of having

Saddam Hussein in power seems almost comforting in comparison with the awful events and wasted effort of America's brave young men and women in uniform, not to mention the $3 trillion and still counting we have spent to build a new Iraq.

In December 2003 and January 2004, I was the first American to conduct a prolonged interrogation of Saddam Hussein after his capture by U.S. forces. I was a senior CIA leadership analyst who had spent the previous five years studying Iraq and Iran. At the start of the debriefings, I felt I knew Saddam. But in the ensuing weeks, I learned that the United States had vastly misunderstood both him and his role as a determined foe of radical currents in the Islamic world, including Sunni extremism.

Ironically, while American neocons tried their best to link Saddam to 9/11 and al-Qaeda, Saddam thought that the attacks on the World Trade Center and the Pentagon would move the United States *closer* to his Ba'athist regime. In Saddam's mind, the two countries were natural allies in the fight against extremism and, as he said many times during his interrogation, he couldn't understand why the United States did not see eye to eye with him. Saddam was a Sunni himself, his Ba'ath Party stood for Arab nationalism and socialism, and he saw Sunni extremism as a threat to his power base. Saddam portrayed himself as utterly fearless, but to my surprise, he told me he feared the rise of extremism in his country. He knew how difficult it would be to use his mostly Sunni apparatus of repression to fight an enemy whose galvanizing principle was Sunni fundamentalism.

The Israeli scholar Amatzia Baram has observed that Saddam was always aware of the danger of a competing elite, regardless of its religious or secular sympathies. Saddam believed that there could be only one leader and said, "You must understand: Iraqis are always plotting against you—especially the Shia!" If you look at Iraqi history since the fall of its monarchy in 1958, you would have to concede that Saddam had a point. Iraqi politics has been beset by rival factions that have often been at each other's throats. Saddam was often mischaracterized as a nonbeliever or as someone who used religion clumsily to promote his own political goals. Actually, he was not hostile to religion per se; he just demanded that he be allowed to control whatever religious activity there was in Iraq. Saddam was a believer, but— and this is a crucial distinction—on his own terms. In 1991, after the Gulf War, he brought religion and religious symbols more and more into Iraq's public life.

But Saddam's religious tolerance had clear limits. As he said to me during his debriefing, "I told them that if they wanted to practice their religion, that would be acceptable to me. But they cannot bring the turban into politics. That I will not permit." Saddam was talking about Shiites, although his injunction applied to Sunni fundamentalists too. In this case, he was referring specifically to Shia religious leaders such as Muhammad Baqr al-Sadr and Muhammad Sadiq al-Sadr, who had chosen to oppose Saddam and threatened his regime with a potential Islamic revolution similar to the one that had overthrown the shah in Iran in 1979. He had both of them killed.

One of the most consequential developments of the past twenty years has been the spread of Wahhabist ideology in the Gulf Arab nations. Wahhabism emanates from Saudi Arabia and seeks to return the faithful to a more austere form of Islam similar to what existed during the time of the Prophet Muhammad. Saddam's understanding of the threat of Wahhabism and his views on the threat of Iranian-inspired terrorism and Iran's ties to Iraqi Shia extremists were particularly cogent and visionary. He saw Iraq as the first line of Arab defense against the Persians of Iran and as a Sunni bulwark against its overwhelmingly Shia population.

However, by the 1990s, Saddam began to see the spread of Wahhabism into Iraq and began hearing about Wahhabist cells being created in his country. During our debriefing of the Iraqi dictator, Saddam said presciently, "Wahhabism is going to spread in the Arab nation and probably faster than anyone expects. And the reason why is that people will view Wahhabism as an idea and a struggle . . . Iraq will be a battlefield for anyone who wants to carry arms against America. And now there is an actual battlefield for a face-to-face confrontation."*

Saddam's removal created a power vacuum that turned religious differences in Iraq into a sectarian bloodbath. For a time, Shiites turned the other cheek to Abu Musab al-Zarqawi's Sunni-led atrocities, hoping to win power at the ballot box. But as the death toll rose, Shiite militias joined the fight.

In December 2010, the democratic uprisings known as the Arab Spring began in Tunisia, and in 2011 spread to Egypt, Libya, Syria, Yemen, Bahrain, Saudi Arabia, and Jordan. Then came the Arab Winter, with a military coup in Egypt and civil wars in Libya, Yemen, and, most consequentially, Syria.

The civil war in Syria began in March 2011 when President Bashar al-Assad ordered military crackdowns on protests against

---

*Debriefing notes, January 13, 2004.

his authoritarian regime. At first the government was opposed by "moderate" Sunni rebels. They were joined a year later by the Sunni Muslim Brotherhood, which was more militant but nothing close to what we would see with ISIS. (Sunnis make up three-quarters of the Syrian population, while Assad's Alawite sect, an offshoot of Shia Islam, represents no more than 10 percent.) By the end of 2013, the conflict had attracted units of al-Qaeda and ISIS fighters, which split in February 2014 over questions of tactics and leadership. ISIS proclaimed its "caliphate" five months later, using videos of beheadings and mass executions—the pornography of violence—to attract thousands of new recruits from the Middle East and the West. The rest is grim history: hundreds of thousands of dead in Syria, half its population of seventeen million displaced, the annexation of large swaths of Iraq and Syria by the ISIS caliphate, and the spread of a multisided war that has drawn in the United States, Turkey, the Iranian-backed Shia militia Hezbollah, and, perhaps most significantly, Russia.

Whether this chain of events would have taken place if Saddam, and possibly his successor, had remained in power is in the realm of counterfactual speculation. Certainly his army would have remained intact, so many of his top officers would not have defected to ISIS and given the jihadists crucial military expertise. He would have used force to keep a lid on sectarian tensions in Iraq. So it could be plausibly argued that, without the U.S. invasion, the Arab world would have remained calm but frustrated under the thumbs of dictators in Iraq, Syria, Egypt, and Libya.

For years, Saddam covertly supported the Muslim Brotherhood in Syria. Did he do this because they espoused principles that he shared? Not really. Saddam did this because the Brother-hood opposed Assad, his rival for leadership of the Ba'athist movement. If Brotherhood operatives had tried to lead an upris-ing against Saddam, he would have quickly moved to crush them.

Saddam was not an intellectual, and he was not someone who understood the larger world. He was especially perplexed by the United States, which he regarded as his chief tormentor. And, in a bizarre way, who could blame him? The U.S. govern-ment was strikingly inconsistent in its attitude toward Saddam, supporting him in the Iran-Iraq War and opposing him in the Gulf War and the Iraq War. This inconsistency was perhaps a key factor pushing Saddam into a series of missteps that eventu-ally placed him on Washington's "must remove" list by the time George W. Bush's administration came into office in 2001. I don't say this to absolve Saddam of blame. Saddam was capable of making mistakes on his own, and when it came to diplomacy or military action, he made some whoppers.

The ancient Greeks understood that when the gods wished to punish you, they gave you your most desired wish. From 1990 to 2003 Washington worked to undermine and destroy Saddam without understanding the potential consequences. We had a poor grasp of how Saddam looked at the world and how he kept in check the smoldering political undercurrents in Iraq. These lacunae eventually came back to haunt the United States during the war and the subsequent occupation of Iraq. Indeed, our lack of understanding reflected a serious flaw in U.S. foreign policy that has plagued us since our founding. The United States usu-ally reacts blindly to threats, whether communism or an Arab strongman, without pragmatically assessing the advantages of engagement and realpolitik. Our leaders seem unable to put themselves in the shoes of foreign leaders, particularly authoritarians.

In 2009, in the first year of the Obama administration, I began reading a book making the rounds in Washington called *Lessons in Disaster*, a fascinating account of McGeorge Bundy's evolving views on America's intervention in Vietnam. It was especially relevant because it appeared just as President Obama was deciding to approve a surge of troops to Afghanistan. I had an added incentive to read it: Bundy was a professor of mine in graduate school and a man I deeply admired. He was a man unafraid to change his mind. Once a hawkish defender of U.S. military actions as national security adviser to Presidents Kennedy and Johnson, he evolved over forty years into a staunch critic of the sloppy thinking that had led us into Vietnam. I was inspired by Bundy's unsparing honesty. Looking back at my thirteen years at the CIA, as a senior analyst at its headquarters in Langley, Virginia, and during eight stints on the ground in Iraq, I noticed a similar evolution in my own views. I was astonished by how much I had revised my early thinking, and I saw clearly some of the errors the United States made in pursuing a war of choice in Iraq when we knew so little about its political and sectarian arrangements.

Saddam had risen to the heights of Iraqi power through sheer will, political acumen, and no small measure of cunning and deceit. Yet he was an ignorant man in some respects, a product of an impoverished youth and a lack of formal education. He killed hundreds of thousands of his own people and launched a war against Iran that took as many as seven hundred thousand lives, one hundred thousand of them civilians. He had used chemical weapons without compunction and deserved the sobriquet "Butcher of Baghdad." Yet he was more complex than he seemed on the surface. It is vital that we know who this man was and what motivated him. We will surely see his likes again in that part of the world.

We try to construct history piece by piece, but we can never say definitively that we have put together a full and coherent story. Remembering and reconstructing events is a painstaking process. Some of the people who played roles deposing Saddam have come forward to tell their stories. But the historical record is far from complete. It is missing, most conspicuously, what Saddam was like in person and what he had to say in the several months after he was captured on December 13, 2003. Because I was with him during that time, and because I had spent years analyzing his leadership, I will try to fill in the gaps as best I can. I hope to help future historians strip away the mythology surrounding this complex man.

People often ask me, "What was Saddam like?" and "Was he crazy?" During the time I talked to Saddam Hussein, I found him to be quite sane. There were any number of genocidal psychopaths around the world, and it was curious that we decided to go after him, especially given the consequences. It is my contention that the U.S. government never gave a thought to what the Middle East would be like without Saddam. Sure, we had heard all the horror stories—the killing of one hundred thousand Shiites in the south and almost as many Kurds in the north after the Gulf War, the use of chemical weapons against Iraqis he saw as political threats, the slaughter of the Iran-Iraq War—but we never integrated these bloody acts with his hugely important role in the neighborhood. We understood this only when he was gone.

When I returned from Iraq in 2004 after my meetings with Saddam, many of my fellow analysts wanted to know what my team learned from him. A few skeptics thought it was all a waste of time. The truth is, we found out a lot about how Saddam ruled and why he did some of the things he did. We also learned a lot of things about the issues that have been used to justify the invasion of Iraq and the toppling of his regime. The most important question—"Should we have removed Saddam from power?"—was never asked or answered. The policymakers at the White House and the leadership on the seventh floor at the CIA didn't want to hear that many of the reasons for going after Saddam were based on false premises. I made repeated attempts to write some version of this story for the CIA's internal use but was met with what can be described only as feigned interest and an attitude of "This is not what we do."

Richard Haass was director of policy planning at the State Department at the time of the Iraq invasion and subsequently became president of the Council on Foreign Relations. He told the journalist George Packer that he never knew why the United States went to war and described the decision as "something that just happened." In his own memoir of the war, *War of Necessity, War of Choice*, Haass describes the three distinct phases of the conflict: first, the policy debate that usually precedes fighting; second, the actual fighting itself; and third, the struggle over the differing interpretations of what the war accomplished and what it all meant. This book represents my contribution to the third part of Haass's analysis. Most of what is said in these pages is based on what I learned during my interrogation of Saddam.

Finally, there is Saddam Hussein himself. He was clearly a threat to U.S. interests in a part of the world that our government defined as vital. He took a proud and very advanced society and ground it into the dirt through his misrule. In the later stages of his rule, he became obsessed with his place in history and was scarcely engaged in foreign affairs. He seemed to want to compensate for his humble beginnings. In many respects, he was similar to the retiree who loves to watch the History Channel. He was fascinated by history but lacked the intellect to learn its lessons. Foreign policy decision-making increasingly passed into the hands of hard-liners like Iraqi vice president Taha Yasin Ramadan, RCC vice chair Izzat Ibrahim al-Duri, and former foreign minister Tariq Aziz. Unimaginative and combative, Ramadan and his circle repeatedly missed opportunities to break Iraq's international isolation. More and more, Saddam was concerned with internal security and his leisure pursuits. In captivity, he would often refer to himself as the president of Iraq, but secondly he would say he was a "writer." That made it very hard to square the latter-day Saddam with his earlier persona as the Butcher of Baghdad.

1.

"Holy Shit, It's Saddam!"

By December 13, 2003, I had been in Iraq for eight weeks. The weather was gorgeous during the day—about seventy to seventy-five degrees—but at night it became frigid and often would rain. It was not unusual to wake up and find a few feet of standing water outside your trailer in the Green Zone. Our military guards finally put down wooden boards as bridges to dry land, creating a walkway to ███████ the building in the CIA compound where we did our classified work and where our computers were.

I was an analyst in the CIA Baghdad station. My job was to help CIA case officers and Army Special Forces target individuals for capture so we could interrogate them for useful intelligence. In the search for Saddam, the most important information came from detainees who might have had access to the Iraqi leader or to his aides. It was painstaking work that entailed keeping in constant contact with the military and our own case officers, running down as many leads as possible, and answering questions from Washington—and from the civilian and military leadership in Baghdad—on our progress in the hunt for High Value Target No. 1, or HVT-1: Saddam Hussein.

The United States had been denied access to Iraq since the Gulf War in 1991. In 2003, I believed the United States had invaded Iraq for the right reasons: to find and destroy WMD (weapons of mass destruction) and liberate the country from a brutal dictator. I believed the WMD threat. Experts throughout government and academia, who had much greater experience than I had, were convinced that Saddam either possessed weapons of mass destruction or was trying to acquire them, a conclusion supported by every piece of intelligence I saw.

As usual, I began the day with the nine-thirty a.m. meeting of the "fusion cell," a group of CIA and military analysts who swapped information and reviewed overnight cable traffic. The ten to fifteen analysts paid special attention to reports that Saddam might have been spotted—we called these "Elvis sightings"—and discussed where new leads might be found. We also made suggestions about who should be detained next in the ongoing effort to pick up Saddam's trail.

We met most days in the annex building ███████████ where analysts from CENTCOM (U.S. Central Command, a combatant command whose theater of operations includes the Middle East) were housed. That morning, we were told by members of the Special Forces that they had a good lead on some key bodyguards we had identified as being close to Saddam. While this sounded encouraging, it was not all that different from a thousand other tips we had chased down over the past several weeks.

After the fusion cell meeting, I read e-mails and intelligence reports and answered queries from Langley on the search for Saddam. Around noon, I went with a fellow analyst, Randy, to Baghdad International Airport to mail some items home. The airport was just outside the Green Zone and was one of the few places where analysts could go without a security escort. It had a post office and a PX where you could buy toothpaste, razors, and other personal effects.

An added attraction was the Burger King restaurant. It was the only place in Baghdad where you could get a taste of home. After the lightning success of the invasion in March, Burger King opened a franchise at the airport to meet the demand of young servicemen and -women who would give anything for a Whopper. In no time, the Baghdad franchise became the busiest Burger King in the world.

Like other service personnel, CIA officers made special trips to the airport, braving the gauntlet of improvised explosive devices (IEDs) for a Whopper and fries. On December 12, after weeks of bland institutional fare, I was desperate for a burger.

But when we got to Burger King, it was closed for lack of food. We had risked life and limb for a Whopper, only to be denied.

On the way back, Airport Road was closed because an IED had been found near its shoulder. Randy and I were diverted from the main road to streets that led us into parts of Baghdad where we had never been before. We had no radio, we were driving an unarmored car, and we were soon very lost. We suddenly found ourselves in a Shia neighborhood as Friday prayers were letting out. The street was a mob scene. Our relatively new vehicle stuck out amid the patchwork-colored cars built from spare body parts. Our flak vests were visible over our clothing, we were both foreigners in a sea of Arabs, and we had no cell phone (I had one of the few functioning cell phones in the station and had left it in my hooch) to call for help if anything went wrong. At one point, I thought we were going to have to ditch the vehicle and swim for it across the Tigris River. But as we drove around, I began to see landmarks that told me we were close to the Green Zone. By the time we finally got back, I was never so happy to see the U.S. military. If this had happened six months later, I doubt we would have been so lucky.

As we got out of the car, I ran into my friend Mike, a National Security Agency analyst on loan to CENTCOM in the fusion cell who was able to tap into sources in the military that were inaccessible to me. He confided that Special Forces troops had captured Muhammad Ibrahim Umar al-Muslit the previous evening. Muhammad Ibrahim, who was head bodyguard for Saddam when he was on the run, broke early and easily. At first he tried to say he was not aware of Saddam's whereabouts. But the lure of the $25 million bounty on Saddam proved stronger than personal loyalty, and he soon led the Special Forces to the former dictator.* (It turned out that Saddam had replaced many of his bodyguards shortly before the fall of the regime. This was a wise move because intelligence agencies all over the world had been studying his security and trying to find ways to pierce it. Saddam was always very careful about his security and usually delegated this responsibility to trusted aides, who were often family members. He was counting on his new praetorians to keep him safe until he could find a way back to power.)

Muhammad Ibrahim took the Special Forces to the very farm where Saddam hid in 1959 after he had taken part in the bungled attempt to assassinate Prime Minister Abd al-Karim Qasim, who had led the coup that resulted in the murder of King Faisal II and the end of the thirty-seven-year Hashemite monarchy. We knew Saddam had been involved in the Qasim plot four decades earlier, but we hadn't known that he had fled to a farm, so hadn't looked there in the nine months he'd been in hiding.

In hopes of finding out more, Mike and I walked to a nearby shed where our special-ops colleagues hung out. But they had suddenly come down with a case of zipped lips. It was clear that the effort to find and capture Saddam was now about who would get the credit. This was something I would have to deal with every time I went to Iraq. The military would go to the CIA for its intelligence expertise and then cut off contact with the Agency when closing in on a target. I called this the "Heisman

---

*Muhammad Ibrahim was subsequently arrested by coalition forces and imprisoned at Abu Ghraib for aiding the insurgency, which gave him deniability for his actions leading to Saddam's arrest. He was later resettled ███████.

treatment," based on the Heisman Trophy pose: a football player with his arm outstretched to fend off opposing tacklers.

It was ironic that the military clammed up on Muhammad Ibrahim Umar al-Muslit, because CIA analysts were the first and foremost proponents of focusing on bodyguards to find Saddam. During the early months after the fall of Baghdad, our colleagues in military intelligence concentrated on questioning the "deck of cards," senior regime figures who were prominent in Saddam's government. Only after it became clear that none of Saddam's senior officials knew where he was did the military go after his bodyguards. The special-ops officers were great guys, and Saddam probably would not have been caught without their heroic work. They attended our fusion cell meetings every morning, were eager to hear our thoughts, and often filled us in on the raids that had taken place the previous night. But now they wouldn't talk about the upcoming round of raids and who was on the target list.

After I left Mike and the special-ops guys, I walked back into the CIA station and felt a buzz of excitement and anticipation that I had not experienced since arriving in Baghdad. Around seven p.m. we received definitive word that the Special Forces were going on a raid they believed would snare HVT-1. Before Thanksgiving, I didn't think we would ever catch Saddam. Finding one man in a country of twenty-six million was hard enough, and it was made doubly difficult by the fact that Iraq was in a state of collapse. Communications technology—such as a functioning telephone system—was pretty much nonexistent. Cell phones were few and far between, and functioning cell phone towers in Baghdad in 2003 were also practically nonexistent. Satellite phones were more plentiful, but not all our counterparts on the U.S. side had them. Internet connectivity was spotty, to say the least, making it difficult to communicate with our colleagues in uniform or our civilian counterparts at the Coalition Provisional Authority, the transitional government created by the United States and its allies after Saddam's fall.

I had spent two months trying to figure out what Saddam might be doing, where he might be traveling, or who he might be meeting with, and I had the sinking feeling that he was a wraith who would forever escape our grasp. I thought how happy I'd be if proved wrong.

That evening, I was at my computer on the second floor of ████████ when Andrew, the chief of the CIA analytic staff, said I was wanted in the chief of station's office. The chief of station was not in the country, so I ended up meeting with his deputy, Gordon, and the CIA's executive director, Buzzy Krongard, who happened to be in Baghdad. Andrew, Steve (who was head of the Detainee Exploitation Cell), and several other CIA officers were also in the room, which was furnished with a large wooden desk and several leather sofas; it was reminiscent of a college dorm, providing a modicum of comfort and showing the wear and tear of hard use. Krongard, a stickler for proper dress, was wearing a blue jacket and a blue sweater. I was outfitted in cargo pants and a hooded Georgetown University sweatshirt. The other men were wearing fleece jackets and jeans.

"If you were going to identify Saddam, how would you do it?" Gordon asked abruptly. "What would you look for?" I said I would begin by looking for tribal tattoo markings identifying him as a member of the Al-Bu Nasir tribe. One was on the back of his right hand between his forefinger and thumb; the other was on the inside of his right wrist. The markings themselves were just a series of dots, some in a straight line and some in a triangular shape, and something that looked like a crescent moon.

While this may seem anachronistic to Westerners, tattoos were essential in Arab countries such as Iraq. Public record keeping was haphazard, and tattoos were a way for tribes to keep track of members. They were a valuable tool for identifying individuals and resolving local conflicts and grievances. For example, if an Iraqi was thinking of taking action against another individual, it was prudent to know his affiliation so as not to risk a wider tribal conflict.

I also mentioned that Saddam had a scar on his left leg from a wound suffered during the attempt to assassinate President Qasim in 1959, and that his lower lip tended to droop to one side, perhaps from a lifetime of smoking cigars—something I picked up from years of studying videotape of Saddam. We were always on the lookout for new footage of him and for signs he might be in ill health. In 1999, I saw video of him in which it was clear he had lost a good deal of weight. This was around the time of Venezuelan president Hugo Chávez's visit to Baghdad. I began poring over recent videos and photographs with CIA doctors. We figured Saddam was simply on a health kick. We were right, but it did not include giving up cigars.

Krongard interrupted me, saying, "We need to make sure this is Saddam and not one of those body doubles." He was not going to tell Washington and the world that we had captured

Saddam until we were absolutely sure the man wasn't a body double. I wanted to yell, "For fuck's sake, there are no body doubles!" But I decided that silence was the better part of valor.

The "body double" notion was the most persistent of the myths about Saddam and was a source of mild disagreement and some humor within the circle of Saddam watchers. Saddam supposedly had men who looked like him and could be used to stand in for him at public gatherings, as well as confuse Western intelligence agencies that might be thinking of assassinating him. This rumor began because, to Western eyes, many of the men who guarded Saddam bore a resemblance to the Iraqi dictator. That much was true. Perhaps it was because many of Saddam's bodyguards were members of his extended family and shared some physical traits. I don't know how many memos were written during the Clinton and George W. Bush presidencies knocking down the idea. But it still cropped up in the memoirs of people like Defense Secretary Donald Rumsfeld and my former boss, George Tenet, director of the CIA from 1996 to 2004.

(Weeks later, during our formal debriefing of Saddam, we asked him if he had ever used a body double. He laughed and said to us, "How do you know you are not talking to one right now? Maybe I am the body double and the real Saddam is hiding." He then threw his head back and laughed heartily. "No," he said, "there is only one Saddam Hussein!")

Gordon told me to be ready in case I was needed to help make the identification. I hurried back upstairs to my computer terminal. Steve caught up with me and told me to come up with a list of questions that only Saddam could answer. Then he said something that would change my career. "We want you to go out and make sure that the guy they picked up tonight is Saddam Hussein." I had been up for twenty-seven hours and was flat-out exhausted, but his words sent jolts of adrenaline through me the likes of which I had never experienced before. I was suddenly the guy who would check off on an announcement that would rocket around the world. I hunched over my computer terminal for the next forty minutes or so, formulating questions for the dictator who had prompted the United States to go to war.

I was told that the military was flying the putative Saddam to the airport that night and we'd make the identification there. A senior CIA officer said we'd meet at the bar before going to the airport. The bar for CIA hands was one of the first things the Agency got up and running in the compound. It was in a trailer and had several TVs, Christmas lights galore, and plenty of cold beer. I used to tell people that if we ran Iraq as well as we ran the bar, Iraq would be the Switzerland of the Middle East. When I got to the bar, senior CIA men were already toasting themselves on Saddam's capture. I waited there for what seemed like forever until I was told that the convoy was at the entrance to the CIA station. I hightailed it back there and hopped into a ▮▮▮▮▮▮.

We drove out on Airport Road shortly before midnight. This was the road that the U.S. media soon dubbed "the most dangerous road on the planet." At night it had become a no-go zone. Just a few weeks before, the ▮▮▮▮▮▮ carrying David Kay, the head of the Iraq Survey Group—the entity established by the CIA at the president's direction to find Iraq's weapons of mass destruction—was ambushed by insurgents on the road. Kay was not killed, but the attack underlined the risks. I wore body armor and carried a weapon. In the ███████ with me were our translator, a man of Lebanese extraction named George; and Bruce, a polygrapher who had a gift for putting people at ease and getting them to talk. (At no time was Saddam given a lie detector test. It was assumed by the CIA station leadership, correctly in my view, that it would insult him and cut off any chance of gaining his cooperation.)

Our drivers were outfitted with night-vision goggles, and we had a small arsenal in the car. We drove with the lights off at upward of one hundred miles an hour, and the driver got us to the airport in record time. GIs with guns drawn stopped us on a side road leading to the Battlefield Interrogation Facility (BIF). After what felt like an eternity, a soldier lifted the crude make-shift gate and we drove down a narrow, unlit path to a series of low-slung blockhouses.

The BIF was a former station for the Special Republican Guard, an elite force of Saddam's most trusted military units, and was located in the first blockhouse. It was pandemonium inside, with GIs rushing everywhere. Standing by a desk were some soldiers armed to the teeth. They checked our IDs and told us to grab seats in an adjacent waiting room, which was outfitted with a large-screen TV, a refrigerator filled with soft drinks, and several sofas. Someone had been watching a DVD of *The Good, the Bad and the Ugly* and had put it on pause, so a single frame from the movie radiated from the screen.

We ended up cooling our heels for several hours, which I spent refining the questions I would ask Saddam. (I would find out later that the Army had already shown Saddam to presidential secretary Abid Hamid Mahmud al-Tikriti and one of Saddam's closest advisers, former foreign minister Tariq Aziz. When Abid saw Saddam, he broke into a grin, presumably because he saw that his boss had been unable to evade the dragnet looking for him, and said, "Yeah, that's him." Saddam, however, did not know he was being watched, because Abid was viewing him through a one-way mirror.) As we waited, a GI walked by with a basin, the kind used for shaving. Someone said the Army had just shaved the Iraqi dictator. At this point, one of our security guys left the room and started following the man with the basin. When he came back, he showed me a zip-lock bag with what appeared to be whiskers in it. He had gotten some of Saddam's facial hair as a souvenir. I thought to myself, "We have got to get this show on the road before more silliness occurs." Finally, a GI poked his head in the room and said, "OK, guys. You're up."

I could feel my heart pounding as we walked down a long, dimly lit corridor. At the end of the hall was a large shower room where Saddam was being held. We stood outside the door for several minutes as military interrogators finished their questions.

Suddenly the door opened and I immediately found myself sucking in air. There he was, sitting on a metal folding chair, wearing a white dishdasha (a long, robelike garment) and a blue quilted windbreaker (it was a cold December night). I had looked at videos and pictures of him for years, and thought to myself, "Holy shit, it's Saddam!" But I realized I had to confirm my gut impression by checking for his telltale markings and asking him questions with, I hoped, revealing answers.

We walked in and took up positions facing him. The place

was packed. In addition to our four-man team (me, translator George, Bruce, and Charlie from the Detainee Exploitation Cell), there were six or seven members of uniformed military in the room. Because I was responsible for verifying that U.S. Special Forces had picked up the right guy, I spoke first (through a translator). "I have some questions I'd like to ask you, and you are to answer them truthfully. Do you understand?" Saddam listened to the translation and nodded in agreement. I first asked him, "When was the last time you saw your sons alive?" Saddam listened and got a wry smile on his face. He then turned back to me and said, "Who are you guys? Are you military intelligence, Mukhabarat [civilian intelligence officers]? Answer me. Identify yourselves!"

I expected Saddam to be defiant, but I was a little taken aback at the aggressiveness of his reply. Before I could answer him, one of our group interjected, "We are not here to answer your questions. You are here to answer ours!" Saddam assented, and we continued with the interrogation. Saddam appeared nonchalant as he listened to our questions. It struck me how quickly he was able to acclimate himself to his new surroundings and his new status as a prisoner. He acted as if he came here every Saturday night and this was a regular part of his routine.

I noticed at once that he had a tribal tattoo on the back side of his right hand, between his thumb and forefinger, and another one on the underside of his right wrist. His mouth drooped as we had seen in photographs and videos. We were well along to a 100 percent confirmation. Now I needed to see the 1959 bullet wound and hear how he answered my questions.

Saddam answered most of the questions truthfully, at least

the ones he chose to answer. He would not say anything about how he had gotten out of Baghdad or who had helped him. He professed not to understand why I was asking him the questions I did. "Why don't you ask me about politics? You could learn a lot from me." I told him I thought that was true, but that I had to ask certain questions first. Normally, I would not conduct an interrogation this way. Anytime a person comes in with a list of questions, you can be certain that the interrogation will go nowhere. A list of questions makes it impossible to establish rapport with a detainee, and the detainee quickly figures out that by saying nothing he can quickly exhaust your questions. However, this was an identification exercise, not a formal debriefing, so I wasn't after expansive answers.

Both the CIA and the military had their own interpreters. I noticed that the military interpreter, a young man wearing fatigues and a khaki T-shirt, would interrupt George (our interpreter) with his own comments. This continued for some time. A question would be asked, or sometimes an answer given, and the military interpreter would say in an authoritative voice, "No, that's not what he said!" or "You have interpreted that incorrectly." We were rapidly approaching a major blowup that would queer the whole debriefing. Saddam watched these exchanges as if he were at a tennis match, his eyes moving from side to side. Soon I saw a little smile appear on his face. He was enjoying this. Saddam began to feign annoyance with our questions and leaned over to the Army interpreter and shook his head. Amazingly, the Army interpreter would often reciprocate. This went on for more than an hour. The tension continued to build, and Saddam just sat back, enjoying the fact that the Americans were not getting along well, which encouraged him to be more smart-alecky. It was fascinating to watch how Saddam could find a small opening and cause friction between people who were ostensibly on the same side. In many ways, the incident was a metaphor for how he ruled his country.

At one point, I asked Saddam if he had anything that he would like to say to us. He said he did, and launched into a diatribe about the rough treatment he had received from the Special Forces unit that captured him. "Is this any way to treat the president of a country? If your President Bush was in the same situation and at the hands of Iraqis, would he be treated the same way? I can tell [you] he would not."

I looked at Saddam with utter incredulity. Here was a man who didn't think twice about killing his own people, yet he was complaining about a couple of cuts and scratches. I told him his complaint would be duly noted. It was true that he had been manhandled by the special operations troops. I remember hearing that someone had punched him and said, "That's for 9/11!"

He began pointing to various cuts and bruises, and lifted his dishdasha to show the damage to his left leg. I saw an old scar and innocently asked if this was the celebrated bullet wound suffered during the attempt to kill Qasim. He assented with a grunt. That was the final piece of proof. We had the right man. We had indeed captured Saddam Hussein.

Someone then asked him a question about WMD. Saddam looked at his questioner and curtly responded, "You found me. Why don't you go find these weapons of mass destruction?" Then Saddam began to warm to the subject of President Bush's fruitless search for Iraqi WMD. Saddam said the Americans were a bunch of ignorant hooligans who did not understand Iraq and were intent on its destruction in the belief that there were weapons when in fact they did not exist. Saddam then got a sheepish look on his face, apparently concerned that he was being rude to his "guests." "I am not speaking about you guys. You seem to be all right. It is your government that I was talking about!"

Finally, someone from our group asked me if I had any further questions. This was my chance to ask the question that I had been thinking about since I saw Saddam's statue being pulled down by U.S. forces in Firdos Square the previous April. "Saddam, I know that you have spent your life building a spot in Iraqi history and that you have tried your best to commemorate your rule with monuments to mark your reign. How does it feel now that all of these statues have been torn down?"

Saddam gave a little laugh. He put up his index finger and said, "I want you to listen to me. I never asked anyone to put up a statue of me. Oftentimes, members of the Revolutionary Command Council would say to me, 'Saddam, we want to put your picture up somewhere or we want to put up a statue of you.' I would tell them no. But the command would overrule me. Who am I to overrule the command?" Again, my jaw dropped because I knew he wouldn't defer to subordinates. As we prepared to leave, I said to him, "Saddam, you mentioned that I could learn a lot from you about politics. I hope we get to have some time to talk politics." Saddam grunted his assent, and we filed out of the room.

We went back to the CIA station as the sun was coming up. Walking back to my trailer, I began to meet people who were just waking up and wanted to know what had happened. One by one, they congratulated me as if I had pulled Saddam from the hole myself. It was very gratifying, but I had been up for thirty hours and all I wanted to do was get some sleep.

Now that Saddam was safely in the hands of the U.S. military, I began to settle into what I thought would be a quiet four weeks until my scheduled return to the States. How wrong I was. A few days later, Rumsfeld said on CNN that the CIA would be the first to interrogate Saddam. My work in Baghdad was only beginning.

2.

"Dare to Be Right"

- - - - - - - - - -

The idea that one day I would be an Iraq expert with the world's leading intelligence agency never crossed my mind, because I never knew such a job existed when I was growing up. I was born on March 8, 1961, on the south shore of Long Island, the youngest of five children. I was a typical kid who had no interest in politics or history or working for the government. I followed sports, and as I moved into high school, I turned my attention to rock 'n' roll bands because that's what my friends and I spent most of our time talking about. I barely noticed the larger world. Having the surname of a disgraced president didn't help stir my interest in government service.

The Middle East was the catalyst for a series of world traumas while I was in junior high school—the assassination of Israeli athletes at the 1972 Munich Olympics, the Yom Kippur War in 1973, the oil embargo of 1973–74—but I was too young to appreciate their significance. When I was in the ninth grade, my school devoted one class, on one day, to the Islamic world. By contrast, we spent weeks on the history and geography of Israel (there were many Jewish students and many who had been taught Hebrew). I didn't give the Middle East a second thought until my brother drove me to the post office so I could register for the draft in 1980. The Middle East was on the boil then—the Soviets had invaded Afghanistan, fifty-two Americans were being held hostage in the U.S. embassy in Tehran, the U.S. embassy in Islamabad, Pakistan, had been attacked—and President Jimmy Carter had reestablished Selective Service registration for all males eighteen to twenty-six years old. It wasn't until 1981 that I even met a Muslim.

I went to Hofstra University on Long Island. I really didn't give it a lot of thought either. I just happened to apply there and was accepted. Hofstra was the perfect place for me. I had great professors, I read a lot, and I fell in love with history, which was my major. I was drawn to Russian history, the evolution of the Soviet Union, and the onset of the cold war. This was the Reagan era and a period of renewed cold war tension. I had little interest in the Middle East.

Reading was the path to my life's work. Two books had a profound effect on me. Robert K. Massie's *Nicholas and Alexandra*, an account of the last tsar of Russia and his family, showed me what happens when an individual collides with the forces of history. *The House on Garibaldi Street*, by Isser Harel, the former head of the Mossad, Israel's secret intelligence service, recounts how the Mossad captured Adolf Eichmann and brought him to justice in Israel. I'll never forget the chilling scene in which Harel confronted Eichmann shortly after his capture, and the Nazi who had organized the Jewish deportations looked up at him and recited the Shma in Hebrew. These books began to pique my interest in the world of intelligence. By my senior year, I was determined to carve out a career in government that would let me see what I had been reading about. I wanted a ringside seat to history.

I went on to New York University to pursue a master's degree in history, with an emphasis on U.S. diplomacy. It was there that I had the good fortune to study under McGeorge Bundy. Once a week we discussed a topic drawn from the cold war. He would give us a synthesis of what had happened and what scholars said about it. He would talk for two hours and not look at a note or even break his delivery with an "ummmm." He had a firm grasp on the latest scholarship and was always willing to take time to meet with students and offer advice—as long as you had an appointment.

In March 1989, I moved to California and got a job as a researcher at an old-line law firm in Orange County. Becoming a lawyer was the default position for twentysomethings, and I thought that maybe I should try to get into law school. Going to California gave me a chance to spend time with my mother and three siblings, who had moved to the West Coast. I also made a lot of new friends. As far as my career was concerned, I probably should have moved to Washington, D.C., and continued along a path to the CIA, but as young people say today, I was living in the moment.

I first applied for a CIA job in 1990, two years after I received my master's from NYU and during the run-up to the first Gulf War. I answered an ad in *Foreign Affairs* magazine and met with a recruiter in El Monte, California. I remember sitting in the waiting room, reading about the invasion of Kuwait and thinking, "Wow. This is pretty big stuff." The recruiter seemed impressed by my answers and said that the next step was taking a standardized test on my knowledge of foreign affairs. I took the test in San Diego. It was an all-day affair—think of the GRE, but for spies. I aced most sections of the test and was asked to come to Washington for an interview. Then the CIA called me and said it needed to postpone the interview. Then I got another call changing the date again. Then another. I finally got a call telling me there would be no interview at all. I was crestfallen. What I didn't know then was that the Agency was entering a period of retrenchment, and hiring had slowed to a trickle.

I moved to Washington in 1993 and began pursuing a second master's degree at Georgetown University's National Security Studies Program. I got my M.A. in 1996 and sent my résumé all over town. In 1997, out of the blue, I got a call from the CIA asking me to come in for an interview. The guards stopped me at the gate, took forever to confirm I had an appointment, and made me ninety minutes late. Walking into the New Headquarters Building, I passed a plaque that read, "And ye shall know the truth and the truth shall set you free." It made me feel that I belonged there. I was desperate to get a job at the CIA.

I was sweating profusely as I sat down with a manager. The interview was conducted in a cubicle where I could hear people on the other side of the flimsy wall. I imagined them laughing into their hands as I strained to sound confident and informed. I was sent home with a polite "We'll be in touch." To my astonishment, I received a call a few weeks later asking me in for a second interview. This one went much more smoothly. After nine months of background checks and lie detector tests, I was given an entrance on duty (EOD) date: February 3, 1998. I was over the moon. My dream of working for the CIA had come true. There was just one catch: No one told me what I would be doing or what subject area I would be responsible for. Just be sure to show up on time on your EOD date!

Just days before I started work, I learned that I would be a leadership analyst on the Iraq account—"Iraq Issue," in CIA parlance—in the Directorate of Intelligence (DI). I was likely given this assignment because I had studied Saddam closely for my master's thesis at Georgetown University. That meant that my primary job would be analyzing Saddam Hussein: the family connections that helped keep him in power, his tribal ties, his motives and methods, everything that made him tick. It was like putting together a giant jigsaw puzzle with small but important pieces gleaned from clandestine reporting and electronic intercepts. "Leadership analysts" focused on the person and his or her relation to the politics of the moment.

I was thrilled by the assignment. I found Saddam fascinating and was surrounded by a great group of people who already had vast knowledge at their fingertips from having worked their respective "accounts" for years. They spoke a language, intelspeak, that was foreign to my ears. Suddenly I was learning about POTUS (the president), SVTC (secure video teleconference; pronounced "civutz"), *NID* (*National Intelligence Daily*), and the PDB (President's Daily Brief), as well as names of the CIA potentates on the seventh floor. I used to tell people it was like watching Spanish-language television without understanding Spanish.

But as with most large bureaucracies, the CIA was governed by lines of authority that were often clogged by people who got ahead by playing it safe and who regarded fresh thinking as a danger to their careers. When I joined the CIA, a theme of my orientation was "Dare to be wrong." As I found out during the Clinton, Bush, and Obama years, the Agency's real operating principle was "Dare to be right."

My managers were the opposite of most of my fellow analysts. They were aloof and distant, unsure of who I was or what I was doing there. They had not hired me and made clear that they wouldn't have if it had been up to them. Why? Primarily because, through a bureaucratic shakeup, they had inherited leadership analysts to their country teams and, though they were not sure what leadership analysis was, were now responsible for the care and feeding of these analysts. My first day on the job they had no desk for me. When they found one, it was in another room away from the rest of the team. In fairness, by the time I arrived, Iraq Issue was dealing with a minor crisis over Saddam's threatening to eject UN weapons inspectors from Iraq, and my managers probably felt they already had enough on their plate. Finding a place for me to sit and work was very low on their list of priorities.

My managers had their go-to people, and it was up to me to prove myself—sink or swim. I knew that the only way to win their confidence was to learn everything I could about Saddam and how he ran things in Iraq. It was a tough slog for the first year, but little by little I began to develop fresh insights into the Iraqi leader. I began to show my superiors that I belonged and, with a little encouragement and some tasks thrown my way, I produced valuable intelligence.

The CIA was woefully unprepared on Iraq, even though it seemed clear by late 2001 that the United States was going to war with Saddam. There was a steady drumbeat emanating from the Bush White House that Saddam represented a growing threat to the U.S. homeland. The Agency responded by beefing up personnel in the Directorate of Intelligence. Over the next two and a half years, Iraq Issue grew exponentially, and a task force mentality took hold. At the CIA, an analytic task force is usually set up to provide support for an administration during times of crises. The task force is designed to provide up-to-the-minute tactical analysis for administration policymakers. What it doesn't do is promote strategic thinking.

My managers claimed to embrace "outside the box" thinking, but they always rushed to the same individuals—usually the people they hung around with on weekends—to provide the same old answers. This lazy thinking was not limited to CIA managers. The CIA staffers who edited the PDB, a compendium of eight to ten one-page memos on various national security concerns, were just as bad. Often they would turn leadership analysis into political assessments, focusing mostly on political currents swirling around a major event and less on what the leader hoped to achieve by a decision or action. They would take a strong piece that looked at a leader's motives or objectives in pursuing a certain course of action and change the story to a

descriptive analysis that addressed country-specific aims, removing the all-important human factor from the analytic content. But once a crisis erupted, every memo that went to the
White House had to have a leadership angle. The president
needed to know everything about his opposite number. We
would hear from White House staffers and even some high-level
officials that they wanted everything we could give them on a
particular leader and his possible intentions. In the case of Iraq
by 1998, the year I joined the CIA, the question changed from
"What is Baghdad up to?" to "What does Saddam want? What
is Saddam up to?"

Iraq was a Hydra-headed account. Saddam's regime was
squabbling with the international community over sanctions and
was in a war of words (and sometimes bullets) with the United
States, which had imposed no-fly zones in the south and north
of Iraq and periodically bombed the country. Iraq had uneasy
relations with all its neighbors, was beset by UN weapons inspectors looking for WMD, and had to contend with feckless
expatriate opponents who mostly lived in the West (or some
neighboring Middle East country) and made grandiose claims
of inside sources and secret armies poised to topple the dictator.
Saddam weathered several coup attempts, some much more serious than a bumbling effort by the CIA in 1996. (That fiasco was
the brainstorm of the Iraqi National Accord, a political party
composed mostly of military and security defectors—and not to
be confused with Ahmad Chalabi's controversial Iraqi National
Congress, which would provide much of the information used to
justify the 2003 invasion. But many of those helping the Agency
were easily uncovered by Saddam's Mukhabarat, the Iraqi Intel-

ligence Service, which learned every detail of the 1996 plot and foiled it in June and July of that year.*)

Managers of the Iraq team always seemed to want the analysts to address the same questions: How stable is the Saddam regime? Will Saddam move north? Will Saddam move south? And where are the WMD? These themes preoccupied George Tenet and his CIA leadership team. Dissatisfied with the "work product" of Iraq Issue, Tenet removed the group's manager and replaced him with a trusted aide named Phil, who would report directly to him.

As a schmoozer, Phil had few equals, and he understood what the seventh floor wanted. He provided simplified material that was easy for policymakers to understand and presented it with the sycophantic touch of an experienced bureaucratic player. This sort of cronyism stifled debate on a highly complex part of the world where religion, culture, and history all jam together. Repeatedly we were asked how we could crack Saddam's regime, what we could do to rattle him, who we could find to replace him. These questions were asked as though good answers were low-hanging fruit. In fact, when dealing with places like Iraq or Iran, an analyst has to go back years and dig through mounds of traffic to get a passable understanding of what might be taking place and what changes would be possible. But to Phil's way of thinking, this crucial background information was useless ancient history. As a consequence, we weren't asking many questions that needed to be answered. (Phil later got his comeuppance

---

*Amatzia Baram, *Building Toward Crisis: Saddam Husayn's Strategy for Survival* (Washington, DC: Washington Institute for Near East Policy, 1998), p. 56.

when he joined the National Security Council staff and ran into Zalmay Khalilzad, who served under President George W. Bush first as deputy undersecretary of planning in the Defense Department and later in three ambassadorships: Afghanistan, Iraq, and then at the UN. Khalilzad distrusted the CIA and often cut Phil out of meetings. Phil was later made deputy head of CIA's Counterterrorism Center, where he worked on combatting al-Qaeda.)

Current intel is the lifeblood of an analyst's work. The daily memos produced for policymakers and other senior officials give them a sense of what's happening around the world (the "what") and what the intelligence community is seeing (the "so what" of an event), so that a busy policymaker has the information needed to do his or her job. But suddenly we were writing more variations on whether Saddam moved north or south and on the whereabouts of WMD. I was the sole analyst on Iraqi leadership, but because I was an untested commodity, I was discouraged from writing about Saddam. So I started to write about his children. I developed the idea that Saddam was grooming his younger son, Qusay, to be his successor, bypassing the elder Uday. The line of succession was of particular interest to the National Security Council and the White House, perhaps a signal in 1998 that the Clinton administration was searching for alternatives to Saddam without going to war with Iraq.

As I look back, I can see that we were severely hamstrung by our lack of resources on the ground. We had no embassy and no eyes and ears in Iraq to tell us what was going on. This made us almost totally reliant on émigré sources. When Muhammad Sadiq al-Sadr was murdered by Saddam's henchmen in February

1999, we didn't know anything about the Sadrists and had almost no idea who Muhammad Sadiq al-Sadr was. A Shia source could have quickly told us that he was a Shia cleric with the rank of ayatollah, a sayyid (someone who can trace his lineage back to the Prophet Muhammad), a prominent political and religious figure in Najaf who challenged Saddam's repression of Shiites, and the father of Muqtada al-Sadr, later the leader of the Shia Mahdi Army and a steadfast foe of the Coalition Provisional Authority. We had never heard of either of them.

Another analyst and I went to Phil to ask if we could write about the dynamics swirling in the Shia world following the death of Sadr. I told our boss that the forces at play among the Shiites would probably help define any post-Saddam government in Iraq. Phil said that policymakers didn't need to know that stuff but encouraged us to keep thinking about it. This was code for "don't waste my time but I don't totally want to blow you off." Without the backing of our bosses, it would be difficult to find out more about this complex target. That highlighted another problem: Our collection of information was so focused on Saddam and his inner circle that any mention of topics that touched only tangentially on the regime were deemed a poor use of resources. In retrospect, it's clear we missed the Shia threat to Saddam's grip on power before 9/11. Largely because of our reliance on émigré groups and opposition figures, many of whom were Sunnis who had nothing but contempt for their Shia brethren, we convinced ourselves that the Shiites didn't matter and that a Sunni strongman would likely be the successor to Saddam.

Even worse, the Agency missed several important developments about Saddam's leadership. One of my colleagues wrote a paper analyzing Saddam's novel *Zabibah and the King*. Her main conclusion was that the story didn't tell us much because Saddam used ghostwriters. Iraq experts knew that Saddam wrote everything himself—his own speeches and now a novel. Yet this analyst asserted that wasn't true because she assumed that a world leader could not possibly have the time to write a novel. Which was just the point. Having time to write it indicated he was not devoting his energies to running the government at a time when war seemed inevitable.

Indeed, in his final years, Saddam had begun to disengage from ruling the country and was mainly occupied with nongovernmental pursuits, his writing chief among them. There was reporting suggesting this was happening, but it was never relayed to policymakers and emerged only after the war. We subsequently found out, as the U.S. military prepared to invade Iraq, that Saddam was sending the latest draft of a novel he was writing to Tariq Aziz to critique. This was not a man bracing for a pulverizing military attack.

Frankly, if we'd had this information in real time and conveyed it to the White House, it would not have prevented the hostilities. The Bush administration was set on war and determined to remove Saddam. But as intelligence professionals, we had a responsibility to pass along this information to policymakers. If nothing else, it might have raised the threshold for going to war. It ranked as a failure almost as great as claims that Iraq had stores of WMD.

Paul Wolfowitz, undersecretary of defense under Donald Rumsfeld, inundated the CIA with requests for information. He was evidently trying to understand the root of Iraq's threat to the United States, but his efforts were often undermined by the silliness of his queries. For example, he frequently asked analysts to comment on stories in *Vanity Fair* or reports on the evening news. My favorite was when he asked my colleagues for their take on an ABC News interview by Claire Shipman with a woman who claimed to be one of Saddam's mistresses. This woman had purportedly gleaned all sorts of revelations about Saddam's WMD programs during pillow talk.

No one was ever able to discern her true identity. We had no records of anyone with her profile having been associated with the regime, let alone as one of Saddam's mistresses. Shame on ABC for even airing such trash, but also shame on the administration for wasting time assessing it. It was just one of the many straws in the wind that the Bush administration pursued in its effort to build a case against Saddam.

3.

Destination Baghdad

I ended up in Iraq somewhat by accident. I loved working on Iraq at Langley, but after three years as a leadership analyst studying Saddam Hussein, I knew that my boss and I would never be on the same wavelength. When the Bush administration took office in January 2001, I decided I needed a change, so I moved to the Iran desk. This proved fortuitous for me, because my former colleagues were inundated with requests from an administration that wanted information only to back up its preconceived ideas about Iraq and Saddam. For most of them, working on Iraq became a nightmare.

In the summer of 2003, the call went out to the various CIA offices that analysts were needed to work in Iraq itself. The first cadres of analysts—many of whom went to Iraq in three- or six-month increments—were finishing their deployments, and headquarters needed to relieve them, a pattern that would be repeated over the next seven years. I volunteered to go because I thought my experience as an Iraq leadership analyst would be useful. I was told that it would be, but that for the time being, I would be posted at Baghdad Airport to review captured Iraqi documents related to WMD. I thought, "Are they kidding? I have a pretty good knowledge of regime dynamics and an understanding of leadership issues. Why are they sticking me out at the airport working on WMD?" I called the person in charge of the duty rosters and reminded her of my background and asked if there had been some mistake. I was told that everything had been carefully looked at and, no, there was no mistake.

But my assignment was radically altered by personnel issues in Baghdad. I learned in late August 2003 that I was needed to replace my friend and former colleague Sean as the analyst for High Value Target No. 1, HVT-1. Sean could not extend his stay in Iraq because of his upcoming marriage in November. The head of the Office of Near Eastern and South Asian Analysis came to me one day and told me she had asked everyone else but no one could make the commitment. "Gee, thanks," I thought, but I assured her that I would go whenever I was needed. I was told to be ready by the end of October. I then began trying to get up to speed on all the things I remembered about Saddam, all the things I had forgotten, and all that had transpired since I had left the Iraq account two and a half years earlier.

I prepared by reading old cables and more recent intelligence. Much has been said about the poor quality of the intelligence concerning Iraqi WMD prior to the invasion. The reporting on Saddam was just as bad. The worst stuff came from Chalabi and the Iraqi National Congress. I dug into some of the leadership analysis done after I left the Iraq desk and was astonished to find that the senior analyst was merely taking some of my old papers and updating them—or merely putting her name on them and recirculating them as fresh. I wondered, How could you hope to understand this very complex man by cutting and pasting work that was almost two years old?

For years at the CIA, I lived and breathed Saddam. When I went to the movies and the film was bad, I often found myself putting memos together in my head. Sometimes I just couldn't stop thinking about him; he was on a video loop in my brain. And I wasn't the only one. I worked with a number of dedicated professionals at the CIA who were as absorbed by Saddam as I was. We had a pretty good bead on the Iraqi dictator, but we hadn't been as perceptive in fitting him into the larger geopolitical picture. I think that as time passed after the first Gulf War and our sources of information dried up, many analysts began to accept the crude caricature of Saddam as an evil butcher who must be stopped at all costs. Thus, it became harder to view him through an empathetic lens, one in which we could see that Saddam faced countervailing pressures that sometimes drove him to a course of action that he pursued at his own risk, such as the persecution of Shia Iraqis who Saddam believed were aiding Iran, a country at war with Iraq. Saddam had to weigh the international condemnation for the way he treated the Shia of southern Iraq against his belief that many in the south were agents of Iran.

Saddam was a murderous Horatio Alger whose brutal methods overshadowed his astonishing rise. He was born in 1937 in Tikrit, then a squalid backwater north of Baghdad—though

Saddam later spent a lot of money on improvements in his home-town. One of Saddam's biographers, Said Aburish, wrote that when Tikritis were seen arriving in neighboring towns, shop-keepers closed their premises because of the Tikriti reputation for banditry and foul behavior. (I've always felt that the intelligence community did not pay enough attention to Saddam's early years and that they were the key to understanding Saddam the man.)

Saddam's father died roughly three months before his birth, and his mother was a clairvoyant, semi-mystical oddball who married her dead husband's brother shortly after Saddam was born. According to the many biographies written about him, Saddam was abused by his stepfather (though he vigorously denied this during our conversations). He was also ridiculed by the other boys in town because his father was dead and his mother was strange. Amatzia Baram, a professor at Israel's University of Haifa and a visiting scholar at several American think tanks, said that young Saddam owned a handgun and would brandish it if he felt threatened. This story became a metaphor for why Saddam was pursuing weapons of mass destruction and why he would never give up this quest. During my time with Saddam, I asked him about this story, and he looked at me as if I were crazy. He said everyone had guns, and if he showed his weapon, it was likely the other person would do the same.

Although never a good student, Saddam was sharp and street-smart. He left his family as a young man and went to Baghdad in search of fame and fortune. In this he was encouraged by his stepfather, who recognized that Saddam would be unable to fulfill his potential in Tikrit. In Baghdad, Saddam moved in with his uncle, Khayrallah Tilfah, the mayor of Baghdad. Saddam and Khayrallah's daughter, Sajida, became inseparable. The union between Saddam and Sajida was a profitable one for Saddam, as it cemented his ties to the powerful and well-connected Tilfah clan and gave him entrée into the world of conspiratorial politics in the Iraqi capital.

Saddam's role in Iraq's revolutionary politics of the late 1950s is murky. He is best remembered for the failed assassination in 1959 of Abd al-Karim Qasim, who had become prime minister after he led an army revolt that overthrew the monarchy. Saddam reportedly started shooting prematurely during the ambush attempt and became wounded in the crossfire of those trying to kill Qasim. Despite his wounds, Saddam made his way out of Baghdad by swimming across the Tigris River and then lived on the run. He pursued his education in Cairo while still a wanted man in Iraq. Then he returned home and helped install the first Ba'athist regime in 1963. Some Iraq experts have claimed that the CIA was complicit in the Ba'athist coup, but I was never able to find evidence of this.

In any event, the fledgling Ba'athist government was ousted from power in 1963. Saddam subsequently spent over two years in prison before he was released by the government of Abdul Salam Arif, Iraq's president from 1963 to 1966. In July 1968, the Ba'athists returned to power in a mostly bloodless coup. Saddam became the vice chairman of the Revolutionary Command Council and was close adviser to Chairman Ahmad Hasan al-Baqr. Saddam took over the internal security portfolio for the government, a job that many in the military thought would soil their reputations. However, Saddam saw it as a way to build his strength in the government and, more important, crush his rivals.

For many years, a key part of the CIA's analytic work on Iraq concerned Saddam's security apparatus and the rings of aides he used to protect him from harm. My colleagues at the CIA—Sean, Jamie, Chris, as well as several other analysts—did seminal work on Saddam's bodyguards. Saddam employed a large (4,500 operatives), layered, and redundant security apparatus. The most senior bodyguards, known as the Murafaqin (companions), controlled the entire security operation. Most of them were Tikritis, and many were related to Saddam. They were the only people, aside from presidential secretary Abid Hamid Mahmud al-Tikriti and Saddam's son Qusay, who knew where the reclusive dictator was at all times.

The second ring was the Himaya, who were responsible for personally escorting Saddam to public appearances and acted as his advance team. The third and fourth rings were the Himaya al-Khas and the Haras al-Khas, respectively; they provided perimeter security and were usually staffed with junior officers. Most came from the Special Security Organization (SSO) and Special Republican Guard (SRG), which had responsibilities beyond protecting Saddam.

Candidates to become Saddam's bodyguards were carefully selected from influential families in Salah ad Din, the province where Tikrit was located. Most of these recruits came from the Bejjat, a group of prominent families who lived in Tikrit and the nearby village of al-Awja and were part of the Sunni Al-Bu Nasir tribe and directly related to Saddam. To become a bodyguard, you had to be nominated by someone within the clan.

The candidates needed to have an unblemished record, underwent a rigorous background check and security screening, were investigated by the SSO, and had to come from a family with attested loyalty to Saddam.

These bodyguards were a cohesive, intensely loyal group whose close associations with Saddam's extended family tended to diminish rivalries and petty jealousies. Saddam encouraged Tikritis to marry other Tikritis and prohibited them from traveling abroad in order to prevent their abduction or recruitment by foreign intelligence services. They were rewarded with lavish perks and consumer goods that most Iraqis only dreamed about. While he was president, Saddam limited his personal contacts to a small group of trusted aides and usually stayed out of the public eye. He conducted his business in secure settings and made sure that his visitors were carefully screened. When we CIA analysts studied Saddam while he was in power, we were always looking to see whether someone close to him might lead a coup against the Iraqi strongman. We usually concluded that it was unlikely that his companions would ever bite the hand that so generously fed them.

Before leaving for Iraq, I went to California to see my family. I was especially eager to see my mother, who had been diagnosed with breast cancer in the late 1990s and was nearing the end of her fight against the disease. I desperately hoped she would be able to hang on until February 2004, when I was scheduled to return from Iraq. The day I arrived in California, she was feeling well and we had lunch together. Then a day or two later, she was suffering a lot of pain. The doctors gave her some pain medication, which was all they could do. It was a tough two weeks. It was almost as if she knew she did not have much time left. She told me that if anything happened to her while I was gone, I should stay where I was and finish the job that I was doing. As I got ready to go back to Washington, she bounced back and seemed to be feeling better. She died in late November while I was in Iraq. There was simply no way that I could have traveled back to the United States in time, and not being able to get home before she passed away is something that will haunt me forever.

I also felt terrible about leaving Barbara, my then girlfriend and now wife. She had put up with my many absences over the years and had never seemed to mind. She understood that was part of the job. However, this time I was going to a war zone and anything could happen. When I think back on it, I was pretty cavalier about the whole thing. I just assumed all would be well. In the summer of 2001, Barbara had been diagnosed with multiple sclerosis, a neurological disease with no known cure. But she never complained and was always upbeat about her chances of recovery. By 2003 she had not really begun to show signs of the disease, so I was sure that she would be all right in my absence. Still, it was very hard to say good-bye.

I arrived in Baghdad in October and was amazed that I had finally made it to Iraq. My group of new analysts were given a short briefing at the airport and then got in vans that would take us to the Green Zone, where the Republican Palace was located. I soon hooked up with Sean, who had worked at the Defense Intelligence Agency (DIA) before we became colleagues at the CIA. He introduced me around and we got to work. Sean briefed me on where the Saddam hunt stood and gave me a list of important streams of reporting that I needed to catch up on.

On my second or third day there, we went to the Republican Palace, which housed the Coalition Provisional Authority, for dinner, and Sean suggested that I say hello to Jane, the former deputy manager of Iraq Issue. When I left Iraq Issue in 2001, Jane and I were not on good terms. But when we greeted each other at the palace, I could tell that our differences had receded, and I was greatly relieved. In a weird twist of fate, Jane would become one of my biggest supporters and a wonderful person to work for. She embraced the concept that to understand Iraq, you had to immerse yourself in the country as much as possible. She had no background in Iraq before arriving as deputy issue manager in 1999, but soon she had developed a good feel for the place. I was fortunate to have had her as a boss.

I also renewed acquaintances with many of my former Langley colleagues, among them my friend Ami, who was always a source of inspiration to me. She was a farm girl from Alabama yet spoke Arabic like a native. She knew that in order to understand Iraq, you had to study its history, culture, politics, and language—and she studied all four.

Time took on a bizarre quality in Iraq. It's difficult to explain, but I felt like the Bill Murray character in the film *Groundhog Day*—that today will be the very same as the day before, and that tomorrow will be exactly the same as today. This phenomenon can be both unnerving and debilitating. I often found myself losing track of time. To break the monotony, every day I went to the gym and walked to the Republican Palace, where Saddam used to greet foreign dignitaries. The change of scenery always helped, if only for a short time.

The security environment had been deteriorating for months. Every day there were new reports of attacks on civilian and military personnel. Before my arrival, the assassination of Ayatollah Muhammad Baqr al-Hakim in August had struck a deep chord with me. The Shia cleric had returned from exile in Iran only months before, and I had written a profile of him for the Agency. He was a charismatic leader who had founded the Supreme Council for the Islamic Revolution in Iraq in the 1980s and had been a student of Muhammad Baqr al-Sadr, who was executed by Saddam in 1980 (Baqr al-Sadr was the father-in-law of Muqtada al-Sadr). The bomb blast that killed al-Hakim as he left a mosque in Najaf also took the lives of at least eighty-four others, including fifteen of his bodyguards. The bombing was attributed to the murderous Abu Musab al-Zarqawi. Just over two weeks later, one of Zarqawi's suicide bombers hit the UN headquarters at the Canal Hotel in Baghdad, killing twenty-two. Far from being over, the war was just heating up.

Shortly after my arrival, I was awakened by the sounds of rockets slamming into the nearby Al-Rashid Hotel one Sunday morning. We also heard reports that insurgents were planning a major attack on the Green Zone on October 31 that was to culminate in deadly suicide bombings. That day started out like any other, but around dinnertime an eerie quiet set in. Sometime between eight and nine p.m., we began to hear shots. People scrambled to get their weapons, but the attack didn't materialize. The next day we learned that Iraq had beaten North Korea in soccer the night before, and jubilant fans had poured out of the sports stadium and indulged in a favorite Iraqi pastime—firing bursts of bullets into the air. (Saddam often took part in celebratory gunfire, so much so that many Americans thought of him as the guy who liked to fire his rifle into the sky.)

After heading into work for the morning meeting of the fusion cell, I usually stayed at my desk until two or three a.m., seven days a week. We lived in trailers, and often four or five of us were packed into each one. Food was sometimes scarce, the power would frequently go out, and there was little to do but work. Occasional mortar attacks broke the routine in a scary way. This was before the Green Zone had fast-food vendors and every organization had its own bar for Thursday-night revelries. I subsisted mostly on Gatorade, Pop-Tarts, and whatever was available at the dining facility, which was usually rice and potatoes. I ate this way because I was afraid of getting food poisoning. If you got sick, there was really nowhere to go but your trailer, and that was too depressing to contemplate. It was better to just keep going on carbs and try to stay relatively healthy until it was time to go home.

Our challenge was not too little information but too much. We were swamped with detailed reports that had to be checked, even though we knew the chances of their panning out were next to nil. Sources said that Saddam was in Basra, that he had fled to Syria (where he had purportedly sent his WMD as well), that he was dressed as a woman and hiding in a Baghdad bus station. Case officers often came to us with details that were at odds with what we knew about Saddam. One day someone from the Coalition Provisional Authority said that a CPA interpreter had been in touch with Saddam's doctor. Naturally, we wanted to know more. We gathered our things and walked over to the CPA offices in the Republican Palace and began searching for the interpreter. Several hours later, when we finally tracked him down, he turned white because he thought he was being arrested. We told him that we had heard that he might have information about one of Saddam's doctors. He laughed and told us he had been at a briefing and had mentioned perhaps we could track down Saddam by finding his medical supply. The thinking was that if we could find the doctor who supplied Saddam's meds, then we could find Saddam. Unfortunately, this turned out to be a dry hole. Things like that happened every day and were a huge drain on our time and energy.

Working alongside me was Mike, a National Security Agency analyst on loan to CENTCOM. Mike had an obsessive curiosity about Saddam, a great store of knowledge, and an infectious sense of humor. No one was better when it came to shooting the breeze about Saddam, passing the time while riding out to Abu Ghraib prison, and keeping cool during a mortar attack. In November 2003 we met with some of Saddam's former bodyguards. We picked them up in a beat-up van with curtains on the side. As we drove through Baghdad, the guards pointed at the safe houses where Saddam used to bed down for the night. They also showed us where the U.S. Fourth Infantry Division had come within a block of Saddam but stopped before they got to his hiding place.

Perhaps the most vexing question, besides where Saddam was hiding, was whether he was connected to Iraq's growing insurgency. At the time, this was a hotly debated issue in the intelligence community in Iraq. Most of the military and some CIA sources felt that if Saddam were captured, the growing insurgency would be decapitated. CIA analysts tried to pour cold water on this theory. We could find nothing indicating that Saddam was linked to the insurgency. Quite the opposite: Zarqawi was creating most of the mayhem and had the sympathy of many Sunnis angry at the CPA's de-Ba'athification program, which removed party members from the military and the government.

I spent a great deal of time debunking some of the sources who claimed to be in touch with Saddam and said that he was directing the insurgents. Not long after I got to Baghdad, a source claimed to have uncovered a plot ordered by Saddam to murder President Bush's daughters, Jenna and Barbara, supposedly in retaliation for the deaths of his own sons in July 2003. Nothing could have been more ludicrous. Saddam was in hiding and had no way of carrying out the murder of two women in the United States. We told Washington that the report had come from a highly unreliable source and was not credible. Even so, the report was disseminated, and a firestorm erupted. We ended up spending weeks trying to conclusively verify or debunk it. It was the kind of scuttlebutt that most knowledgeable Iraq hands just laughed at. But Washington believed it to be true, perhaps because it fit the caricature of Saddam. We never found anything that even remotely supported the idea of an attack on Bush's daughters.

I worked with one case officer, Dave B., who really did have a good understanding of the regime, spoke good Arabic, and had identified a former regime official named Muhammad who we believed could help us find Saddam. We met with Muhammad several times before the climactic night of December 13. He said Saddam was in hiding near Tikrit. In order for him to help us find Saddam, Muhammad wanted money and a car and said he would be in touch. The most important thing he said was something that nobody else had picked up on: He said that people were tired of sheltering Saddam and wanted to get on with their lives. It showed us that Saddam was running out his string. To this day I believe that, given a little more time, Muhammad would have led us to Saddam. However, more important leads soon developed to uncover Saddam's hiding place.

Saddam's driver, whom we can call Samir, had been imprisoned by the time I arrived in Iraq. Sean and I questioned him in early November to see if we could get any clues about where Saddam might be holed up. Samir said that he had left Saddam shortly after the dictator had fled Baghdad and that he'd subsequently lost track of him. Young and slight of build, Samir seemed an unlikely Saddam bodyguard. But he was highly trusted by Saddam, and a favorite Himaya. I first laid eyes on him on CNN right after the regime fell. Saddam was going through the streets of Baghdad saying good-bye from atop an automobile. When he got in the car, Samir was behind the wheel.

From our talks with Samir we learned much about Saddam's early days on the run. During one of their first nights after leaving Baghdad, Samir pulled up to a house and Saddam instructed him to ask the owners if they would put him and his guests up for the night. An old woman answered the door and declined the offer. When Samir mentioned that the president was asking only for a place to sleep, the woman berated Samir for arriving later than was appropriate to receive guests. According to Samir, Saddam was amused by the woman's punctiliousness.

Saddam then went to Ramadi along with his sons, Uday and Qusay, and the presidential secretary, Abid Hamid Mahmud al-Tikriti. Samir made his way to the compound of a prominent Sunni family friendly to Saddam, and the group took refuge there for several days. Saddam moved on after a cruise missile hit the compound very close to the building where he was staying.

Saddam's group proceeded north toward Tikrit. After a day or two of travel, Saddam decided it would be best if the group split up. Uday, Qusay, Abid, and a few others headed toward the border with Syria to seek asylum. This was remarkable to many in the intelligence community who thought Uday and Qusay hated each other. Uday, supposedly jealous of his brother's elevation as heir apparent, thought Qusay was spying on him and reporting back to Saddam. By 2003, Uday was severely crippled by his injuries from the unsuccessful assassination attempt on him in 1996 and had serious substance abuse problems. Qusay could have left him and saved his own life as well as the life of his son, Mustafa. However, Qusay stuck with his brother, and the three of them were killed by U.S. forces at a sheik's house in Mosul on July 22, 2003.

Saddam's decision to split up his group was a fascinating

twist in his flight from Baghdad and gave us an early clue as to how he would behave. Despite being the father of the two young men, Saddam chose to go it alone. Uday's inability to walk hindered the group's flight and made the men conspicuous to coalition forces. So rather than maintain the family bond, Saddam entrusted his sons' care to his secretary. Abid was captured while traveling to tell Uday that ███████████████████████ for a short while. Several weeks later, Abid's captors brought him to a morgue to identify Uday and Qusay. ████████████

████████████████████████████████████

████████████████████████████████

The haphazard nature of the flight fascinated analysts. There was no master plan, no underground passages to special airfields, no planes waiting to whisk the Iraqi leader to safety and sanctuary. It was almost as though Saddam calculated that if he didn't have a plan, his enemies wouldn't know where to look for him and his friends couldn't betray him. Saddam was right, at least when it came to fleeing Baghdad. █████████████

████████████████████████████████████

████████████████████████████ Saddam refused to comment.

████████████████████████████████████

████████████████████████████ The DIA maintained that there was a labyrinth of underground tunnels used by regime elites—and also used for hiding WMD. This claim was based on satellite imagery. The CIA maintained that there were no underground transportation arteries designed to facilitate regime leadership flight from the capital. After the invasion, it was revealed that the secret tunnels were just a series of revetments along the roads at the airport.

Samir told us that he had left Saddam near Tikrit and had promised to come back to him. ▮▮▮▮▮▮▮▮▮▮▮▮

Saddam's favorite dish was *mazgouf,* an Iraqi specialty of grilled fish and a staple of Iraqi cuisine. Samir also told us how strong Saddam was and how, when everyone else was exhausted, Saddam would have boundless energy. Samir said he had told us everything; he just wanted to see his wife and children again.

In fact, Samir knew full well where Saddam was. At the Tikrit farm where Saddam had fled were a caretaker, his wife, and another young man. We later found out that the young man was Samir's best friend. Samir was lying and nothing could make him divulge the information that we needed. Not even twenty-five million dollars. Not promises that his help would be looked on favorably. Nothing worked, because Samir loved and feared Saddam and worried what might happen to himself and his family if Saddam, who was still on the loose, knew that he had informed on his hideout. Yet Samir took a lie detector test and passed with flying colors. "I really think he's telling us the truth," Jim the polygrapher said. I often wondered if he'd actually administered the test or was just telling us that he had. Resources were at a premium, and those of us looking for Saddam were always running up against colleagues seeking intelligence on the growing insurgency who were making claims on the same resources. The twin issues of hunting Saddam and fighting the insurgency were not synonymous and forced analysts and operatives to have to decide which was more important for American national security objectives. More times than not, collecting information on the insurgency won out. Sometimes people were not above lying.

Samir had been convincing about not knowing Saddam's current whereabouts, but something was nagging at me. Call it intuition. I could not get rid of the feeling that he was holding back on us. Time and again in Iraq, I found that if someone was determined to not tell you the truth, it was very difficult to wheedle it out of him. You have to come up with strategies for extracting information, and that takes resources and personnel—drivers, security guards, translators, polygraphers—that were in short supply. I'm proud that I was never involved in any of the coercive practices approved by the Agency, such as waterboarding. I never saw any evidence that coercion worked.

When I later asked Saddam about why he refused to answer our questions about the help he received after fleeing Baghdad, he insisted that he had not fled at all. He said he merely changed his location so he could continue to oppose the occupation of his country. When I asked why he would not discuss the people who helped him, he responded with incredulity: "These are my friends. Why should I tell you and endanger their safety? Besides, I might need their help again someday!" I marveled that he still thought there was a way out of his predicament. He was delusional, but also steadfastly loyal to the people who had been loyal to him.

4.

Winging It

Debriefing Saddam Hussein was a challenge, especially for the first team in. He obviously was not happy about his predicament and was constantly trying to wrest control of the debriefings from us. After a few weeks, we were able to build a measure of rapport with Saddam, and he began to accept the conditions of his new surroundings and his confinement. This gave a head start to the debriefing teams that came later. Saddam could be remarkably forthright when it suited his purposes. When he felt he was in the clear or had nothing to hide, he spoke freely. He provided interesting insights into the Ba'ath Party and his early years, for example. But we spent most of our time chipping away at layers of defense meant to stymie or deceive us, particularly about areas such as his life history, human rights abuse, and WMD, to name just a few.

Saddam was tough, shrewd, and manipulative. He was a keen judge of his interlocutors, constantly looking for vulnerabilities that would give him an edge. He was all about control—not only in the debriefings but also when it came to his guards, meals, medical checkups, and the conditions of his imprisonment. Because he would push back against any obvious efforts to manage him or challenge his sense of control, we shamelessly appealed to his vanity and asked questions in roundabout ways, ████████

██

██████████████████████████████████

Saddam was, for the most part, attentive and able to discuss a wide range of topics. At times, it was frankly hard to shut him up. He loved to talk, especially about himself. But when confronted with his responsibility for Iraq's misfortunes, he became upset and gave us angry looks. On topics in which self-incrimination and personal responsibility were not at issue, his memory could be razor-sharp. At times I would ask him an obscure question, or show him a picture taken twenty-five years before, and his response would be exact and detailed. Unlike most prisoners, he didn't seem particularly disturbed by the confinement itself, perhaps because of his previous two-year imprisonment (from 1964 to 1966) or perhaps because his life as president of Iraq was so regimented that it almost felt like a prison. He showed no signs of anxiety, confusion, paranoia, or delusion. At times, he even displayed a self-deprecating sense of humor and occasionally broke out in a shoulder-shaking chuckle. He often answered questions with his own questions or gave answers in the form of parables. More often than not, he would let his questioner decide what he was saying, instead of explaining it. He was not cosmopolitan; his statements and demeanor reflected his impoverished, rural, tribal Tikriti background. But these putative weaknesses were the source of his instinctive and deep understanding of Iraqi society and the levers of power needed to control it.

The initial ████████ assessment of Saddam suggested that he was a chronic liar. ██████████████████████████

██

██

██

██

██

██

██

██

██

██

██

██

██

████████████████████████ But not everything Saddam said was a lie—far from it, in fact—and I believe his ████████ pro-filer was mistaken about him. There was a predisposition on the part of almost everyone handling the Iraqi dictator to blow off everything he said, unless he miraculously admitted to having WMD or ordering genocidal attacks. Saddam could be quite candid when he chose to be. However, our preconceived ideas about him sometimes got the better of us. We would at times hammer away at an issue, feeling as if we were making no progress when in fact we were. One time, we asked about his relations with neighboring leaders, and Saddam began to give his unvarnished opinions, mostly negative, about King Abdullah of Jordan and President Bashar al-Assad of Syria. The next day, when we continued our discussion, Saddam said, "I think I said too much yesterday. So now I will say nothing." I sometimes wondered if Saddam knew how well he concealed things, or if he consciously exploited the Western depiction of him as the devil incarnate.

When, a few days after Saddam's capture, Donald Rumsfeld said on CNN that the CIA would be the first to debrief Saddam, it sent a shudder through our ranks. Up to then Saddam's whereabouts had been kept secret, but by singling out the Agency, Rumsfeld came dangerously close to giving the game away. We were worried that our daily travel to and from the airport might lead watching eyes to presume that something important was taking place near there. Saddam was being held at the Battlefield Interrogation Facility (BIF), the old Special Republican Guard facility near the airport that was now used to house prisoners after they were picked up off the battlefield. While that might not have worried Rumsfeld, it was a major concern for us and Admiral William McRaven, who was in charge of Saddam's care and general well-being. Despite the fact that Saddam was never going to escape from his incarceration, his safety was less certain. His cell was close to a main road, in easy range of rockets and mortars. And of course his CIA interrogators would be right in the line of fire.

As we began to get ready to debrief Saddam, the Agency decided to include a polygrapher, Bruce, in the interrogation sessions, along with me and an Army interpreter, Captain Ahmad, who was of Palestinian descent. Bruce wasn't there to administer lie detector tests. The Agency thought his style of ingratiating conversation might loosen up Saddam. Bruce knew virtually nothing about Iraq, and he had to ask me to come up with topics to discuss with Saddam. I said there were many things to talk about, but if we didn't have detailed knowledge of Saddam's story, the sessions would likely not be fruitful.

When I explained this to Bruce, it occurred to me that our government had never prepared for capturing Saddam alive. U.S. officials took it as a foregone conclusion that Saddam would kill himself rather than be captured, or be killed as he tried to escape. When he was captured alive, no one knew what to do.

During the first week after Saddam's capture, we waited for guidance as policymakers dithered over how they should handle the new detainee, and valuable time was lost in seeking information from the former dictator. Almost anyone with experience in questioning prisoners will tell you that the first twenty-four to forty-eight hours are crucial. That's when the shock of capture is freshest and when the altered nature of a prisoner's surroundings and his new status as a detainee can lead him to divulge valuable information. Once the shock wears off, a prisoner begins to feel comfortable and confident in his surroundings, and the interrogator's job becomes more difficult. Rapport building is essential in most interrogations, but can be time-consuming. Thus any information that can be immediately gleaned after capture can save time down the line.

One night I sat down with Bruce and talked about the work I had been doing as the analyst charged with helping track down Saddam. We commiserated with each other about the slapdash nature of what we were about to embark on. The CIA had told us to get ready to interrogate one of the twentieth century's most notorious dictators, but we didn't know how much time we'd have or when the debriefings would start or end.

I mentioned to Bruce that when intelligence officer Kim Philby defected from Britain to the USSR in 1963, his KGB handlers debriefed him over a two-year period. Likewise, when Nazi war criminal Adolf Eichmann was kidnapped by the Israeli Mossad in 1960 and brought to trial in Jerusalem, the debriefing process produced more than 3,500 pages of text and a 127-page memoir written by Eichmann himself. (I had wanted to ask Saddam to do the same, but his military guards refused to give him writing utensils for fear that he would use them to harm himself.)

Bruce and I talked for three hours about Saddam, his history in office, his biography, what motivated him, and what approaches might get him to talk. I could tell from the way Saddam acted on the night we confirmed his identity that he would try to play us against each other. What made our job exponentially more difficult was the fact that we had no carrots or sticks to use in getting him to talk. Originally, the head of our team wanted to take an aggressive approach of stripping him naked and pouring cold water on him, a tactic that had been used to some effect on prisoners ███████████. This was a bad idea. I thought it would be humiliating for Saddam and strengthen his resolve not to tell us anything of consequence. Fortunately, it was nixed by the seventh floor at Langley. Shortly after his capture, Saddam was granted POW status, which gave him the protections of the Geneva Conventions for wartime prisoners. Word also came back from headquarters that the United States wanted him treated according to "Geneva Conventions plus." This meant that no coercive measures of any kind were to be used during his interrogation. In fact, the Agency felt uncomfortable with the whole notion of calling them "interrogations." They wanted us to "debrief" Saddam.

About the only guidance we got from Langley was that the FBI would be arriving someday in the not-too-distant future and that we were to get as much information as we could before turning the debriefing over to the Bureau. Headquarters had sent us a list of questions for the Iraqi dictator, many of which weren't terribly pressing. The seventh floor was primarily interested in where Saddam had hidden his weapons of mass destruction. This would become a point of contention between Saddam and us.

The only topic put off bounds was terrorism. That was reserved for the FBI, which would try to build a criminal case against Saddam based on his alleged links to international terrorism and to crimes committed against the United States. Where the case could be brought was a matter of conjecture, and there were problems with the three possible alternatives. Saddam could be tried by the International Criminal Court, but this was not likely because the Bush administration did not recognize its jurisdiction. He could be tried by an Iraqi court, something that did not exist yet, and the only Iraqi legal code at the time had been written by Saddam's Ba'athist party. Or he could be tried in the United States, an option that was eventually rejected by Washington. Whatever the venue, the prosecution would use information from the debriefings as evidence against Saddam, and the U.S. government wanted to make sure that people familiar with the legal process, namely the FBI, gathered evidence that would stand up in court.

A few days after we began debriefing Saddam, the CIA sent one of its lawyers to give us the ground rules for how Saddam was to be handled. When the lawyer arrived, he asked us how things were going. I said that we'd had only one session with Saddam and that he hadn't said anything of value on the key issues of human rights abuses or WMD. The lawyer said, "Good. The less he says to us, the better. If he says anything of substance, then we will have to document it and you will have to appear in court." I was mystified. First we were told to keep Saddam talking, and now we were told to make sure he didn't say anything of value. The Agency lawyer said that the last thing we wanted was to appear in open court. So now our guidance was simply to keep the process of discussion with Saddam continuing, but only in the hope that he would not say anything incriminating until the Bureau was ready to take over. I looked at Bruce, and he returned my look with a quizzical "Huh?"

On December 20, a week after Saddam's capture, our team went to the airport to see where we would debrief Saddam. We arrived at the BIF and introduced ourselves to the U.S. military men there. I remember thinking that if they ever made this into a Hollywood movie, the setting would be a sleek underground facility with moving walkways, floor lighting, and state-of-the-art recording facilities. In reality, the interrogation took place in a bare room with some plastic chairs inside a dingy guardhouse. The military had rigged up a microphone and a small peephole camera to broadcast the proceedings to others in the room next door—which led to dozens of requests from would-be gawkers to get a glimpse of the proceedings, most of which were denied. After we took a look around, my team leader, Charlie, asked me for my cell phone—he wanted to call the Chief of Station ██ ███████—and went outside. Charlie was in charge of overseeing the whole debriefing process, from daily "sitreps" (situation reports) to finished intelligence reports (known as TDs) that were gleaned from the questioning. But he didn't sit in on the questioning.

He came back a few minutes later and told us that headquarters wanted to start the debriefings right away. There would be no preparation, no time to go over our game plan, no time to decide what subjects to bring up first. We were just going to wing it. And the sooner, the better, because the object was to cram in as many debriefings as we could before the FBI replaced us. I looked at Bruce, and we just shrugged and walked down to the debriefing room.

We arranged ourselves in the debriefing room and prepared for Saddam's entrance. There was one empty chair for the deposed dictator. Suddenly the door opened and Saddam entered, wearing a hood and holding on to the arm of the GI who guided him in. The hood was removed and Saddam looked around the room very quickly, taking it all in. He looked the same as he did when I saw him on the night of his capture. He wore a blue quilted jacket and a dishdasha. His hair was long and he needed a shave. He paused to make eye contact with each of us, moved toward us and smiled warmly. He shook our hands and said hello like a Boston pol working the room. (A few years later I went to see the film *The Last King of Scotland*, about the Ugandan dictator Idi Amin. In the film's opening scene, Amin is injured in a car accident and is treated by a physician who happened to be passing by. Initially, Amin reacts with caution as the unfamiliar doctor gets close to him. But soon he is laying on the charm and trying to win him over. I got a sudden rush of déjà vu. This was exactly the way Saddam reacted when meeting us for the first time.) Whatever his atrocities, there was no denying that Saddam had great charisma. He was a big man, six-feet-one and thickly built. I am six-feet-five but Saddam seemed oblivious to the difference. He was a man who had an outsize presence. Even as a prisoner who was certain to be executed, he exuded an air of importance.

Bruce made introductions and, before I knew what was happening, introduced himself as Mr. Jack and me as Mr. Steve. When I asked him later why he did this, he said it was for my own protection. From then on, I was known to Saddam as Mr. Steve. This was fine, except for the day when I had my coalition ID badge hanging around my neck. I saw Saddam looking at the badge, and I could tell he was trying to read it. I was able to take it off, but then Saddam erupted: "Who are you? What are your names? I want to know now!" This was a constant refrain from Saddam: Who were we, really? We never told him exactly who we were. We just said that we represented the U.S. government and that we were sure that he already knew what organization we belonged to. Saddam finally got a grin on his face and said, "OK, I get it."

I was a bit tongue-tied in the first couple of sessions with Saddam. After studying history for so many years, I now found myself in the middle of it. When you're a leadership analyst at the CIA, you're always at a remove. Saddam was a man I knew from photographs, from biographical anecdotes, from researching his family ties, from descriptions of Iraq defectors, from clandestine reports on his leadership style and autocratic excesses. Now he was sitting across from me.

The first session was designed to get Saddam talking. We did not ask any hardball questions because we were still feeling him out. We had to win his trust, or at least his tolerance, because we had nothing to offer him in exchange for his cooperation. We could not tell him that we would speak with the judge and ask that his sentence be reduced. We had no idea how Saddam would be prosecuted or who would do the prosecuting.

We told him that we wanted to discuss the events of his regime with him. We stressed that policymakers in the United States were very interested in what he would have to say. I held up a number of books with Saddam's picture on the cover. I told him that there was a lot of information about him in the West. Some of it was accurate, some of it was inaccurate, and some we simply were not sure about. I told Saddam that this was his chance, once and for all, to set the record straight and tell the world who he was. Saddam listened and nodded his assent.

Ahmad, our interpreter, was enormously valuable. Being the only Arabic speaker in the interrogation facility, Ahmad had chatted with Saddam even before we started our debriefings. He filled us in on some of Saddam's doings between the night of his capture and our first interrogation. He said that Saddam had acclimated himself pretty quickly to his surroundings and had seemed fairly humble, one time asking for a needle and thread so that he could repair his clothes.

After a day or two of captivity, Ahmad said, Saddam had asked him, "How come nobody is coming to talk to me?" This was very encouraging news. Up to then, we had no idea if Saddam would be willing to talk with us. To be honest, we didn't know what to expect. He had been pretty combative the night of his capture, and we had to be prepared for anything. After the interrogations began, Ahmad stayed with Saddam when the doctors came to perform routine checkups. Ahmad reported on how Saddam was feeling and what he said about the things we had talked about.

Our debriefing of Saddam should have been carried out over months, not days or weeks. After the first few sessions we spoke with our team leader about this. We said that the interrogation needed to be handled in a methodical way. We thought we could gain his confidence, but only if we were given enough time. The response was curt: "This is the plan. The FBI will be out here in a few days. We have him until then. Find out what you can." There was nothing about checking back with CIA headquarters, nothing about coming up with a plan that specified our objectives. Everything had to be done on the fly. We learned a lot from Saddam, but we could have learned a lot more. As Saddam would have said, "The spirit of dialogue was not there."

Our military colleagues could not have been more helpful. Led by McRaven, they went out of their way to help us with everything we needed. When the unit's doctor balked at giving us Saddam's daily medical chart, we asked McRaven to intervene. The next morning, the physician gave us up-to-the-minute data on Saddam's medical condition. McRaven was a stellar officer and a natural leader, and I wasn't surprised years later when

I learned he had organized the raid that led to the death of Osama bin Laden.

During our first couple of sessions, Saddam seemed to become comfortable with us and even enjoy our conversations. One time he told Ahmad the interpreter that he wanted to use the bathroom before our session so that we would not be interrupted. Once he asked for a new dishdasha because "he wanted to appear more presentable." Often at the end of our sessions he would say something like "I told you more than I thought I would," or "We could probably have very good talks if we were to meet outside these circumstances."

But at other times, Saddam was confrontational. During our third session, he began an answer to one question by saying, "I am Saddam Hussein al-Tikriti, president of Iraq. Who are you?" Another time he got so upset by my questioning that he refused to shake my hand and just sneered at me. He then put on his hood over his face and angrily lifted his arm to the guard to guide him out of the room.

Saddam believed the world needed to know Iraq's history, all the way back to Mesopotamia, to understand that the things he did were what he had to do, because of who he was and where he had come from. Saddam had a grand idea of how he fit into Iraq's history. He saw himself as the personification of Iraq's greatness and a symbol of its evolution into a modern state. "Historians are like people who could see through the dark," he said.

At our first session, I said that it was important to know what had happened one hundred years ago, and Saddam scoffed at me. A thousand years ago, he said, correcting my shortsightedness. He then asked us if we had heard of Saladin, the great Iraqi warrior. Bruce, in an attempt to draw him out, told him no. Saddam's eyes grew large and, with incredulity in his voice, he said, "Oh, but you must know who Saladin was. He is very important." To which the polygrapher said, "Well, why don't you tell us about him." Saddam launched into a long exposition about Saladin's victories and enemies. He recounted how Saladin had retaken Jerusalem from the Crusaders. Saddam felt a strong kinship with the great warrior. He also was proud that Saladin was from Tikrit. What he didn't mention was that Saladin was a Kurd.

Saddam said that if we wanted to discuss history, he would be happy to talk with us. At this point his voice grew stern, he raised his index finger, and he said with great conviction and a sharp edge that he would not submit to interrogation. We said that was not our intention. Of course, that was exactly what we planned to do. To get at the questions we really wanted answered, our plan was to introduce subjects that were congenial to him and try to get him talking. We would put chum in the water and hope he took the bait.

5.

Getting Under

Saddam's Fingernails

We began with a history-related question at our fourth session, asking Saddam to name his favorite world leaders. He thought long and hard about this. His answers were surprising. He said he most admired de Gaulle, Lenin, Mao, and George Washington. They were all founders of political systems, and Saddam felt a kinship with them, perhaps because he had shaped modern Iraq and what was known to scholars as the Ba'athist Party. It was notable that he didn't mention any Arab leaders. Saddam said he particularly liked the French: "I had traveled there twice and had gotten to know the mayor of Paris, Jacques Chirac, quite well. I had intended to go back, but then the wars started, and who has time to travel when your country is at war." When we asked him about his relationship with Chirac, Saddam said that he didn't understand him. He thought they were friends, but Chirac did not come to help him. Saddam had relied on France, a permanent member of the UN Security

Council, to support his efforts to get out from under international sanctions. However, the French were never able to support Saddam to the extent that he felt he deserved. During this exchange, Saddam made a sweeping gesture with his upper thigh, as though he were wiping away something unpleasant.

When I mentioned the USS *Stark*, Saddam suddenly grew quiet. Until this point, he seemed to be enjoying himself. Now he affected a lack of interest and chose to say nothing. I kept pressing him. In May 1987, during the Iran-Iraq War, the Iraqis mistakenly fired Exocet missiles at the USS *Stark*, which was in the Persian Gulf protecting international shipping. I told Saddam that some U.S. analysts felt the attack on the ship was deliberate, an attempt by Saddam to get even for the Iran-Contra episode, in which the United States secretly sold arms to Iran via Israel, Saddam's two most determined regional foes during the Iran-Iraq War. Saddam refused to look me in the eye. He began to nervously play with his hood, picking off invisible pieces of lint and folding and refolding the fabric. This was very unusual behavior and something we would see again whenever uncomfortable topics were introduced. In the language of experienced interrogators and psychiatrists, it was a revealing nonverbal cue.

Saddam tried to act as though Iran-Contra had not soured him on the United States. However, it was clear that he was deeply disturbed by what he saw as American double-dealing with his enemy during a bloody war. Years later, at a briefing at

Langley, Charles Duelfer, the WMD hunter, tried to argue with me that Iran-Contra was not a significant event in Saddam's career. He produced a timeline with milestones in Saddam's relations with the United States. I asked why 1986, the year Iran-Contra was disclosed, wasn't on the list. Duelfer became visibly agitated when we spoke about it.

The opening to Iran had occurred in the mid-1980s, during the years of our simultaneous development of good relations with Baghdad. The United States had given Saddam credits and loans, had shared intelligence with Iraq on Iranian troop movements, and had reopened an embassy in Baghdad in 1984. (Memories of the 1979–81 hostage crisis at the U.S. embassy in Tehran were still fresh. Iran was viewed as implacably radical and, unable to get credits from abroad, had to pay cash for arms during the Iran-Iraq War.) In the Iran-Contra report that was published in 1987, Saddam learned that one of Iran's negotiating conditions was that Washington help overthrow Saddam's regime. This was the first mention of regime change in Iraq, fifteen years before George W. Bush officially made it the policy of the U.S. government. In 2011, my view of Iran-Contra's importance to Saddam was vindicated by the publication of secret papers recovered by the U.S. military after the invasion. They included minutes from the Revolutionary Command Council meetings in which Saddam discussed Iran-Contra. As Michael Gordon wrote in *The New York Times*, "The Iran-Contra affair proved to be particularly bitter for Mr. Hussein and his aides, and they struggled for weeks to comprehend it. Among other things, they could not understand why the Reagan administration had taken military action against Libya in 1986 but was reaching out to Iran, since, Mr. Hussein said, Iran 'plays a greater role in terrorism.'"

We spoke for two and a half hours and suddenly we heard a knock on the door. It was time for Saddam's dinner. We all stood up and said that we would be back soon to talk to him. Saddam nodded his head in agreement. He turned to leave and then turned back to face us. He put his hand over his heart and said, "I would like you to know that I have really enjoyed this. It has been months since I talked with anyone. It has been so long since I have been able to have a meaningful conversation and I look forward to our next meeting." He smiled and turned his back to us as the hood was put over his head and he was led back to his cell. We all almost fell over. We were highly encouraged by Saddam's affirmation of our effort and hoped it would lead to a productive debriefing process. We immediately conveyed to Langley that Saddam seemed willing to expand the scope of our conversation. Despite our pledge to talk only of "history," we would soon roll into our questions about the regime.

We got back to our trailer and began to write up our notes. Soon we were visited by the chief of station, a man named Bob, who came out of the National Clandestine Services (NCS), the CIA's operational arm. He had no Middle East experience and supposedly had been brought in to whip the Baghdad operation into shape. Like many members of the NCS, he had a very low opinion of analysts. The case officers from the NCS professed not to know what analysts actually did. You would try to explain your job to them and they would act even more confused. The case officers were extroverts—confidence men, really—who would cozy up to analysts to tap our expertise when they were vetting a source.

Members of NCS also thought that analysts were the source of leaks to the media. Bob told me that if I so much as breathed a word of what Saddam said, I would be removed from the debriefing team. Clearly, Bob did not like the idea of having an analyst as part of the team, perhaps for reasons stated above. That night he told me that I would no longer be in the room with Saddam and that Charlie, our team leader, would handle the debriefing. When the questioners were finished, I would write up the daily report based on what they told me Saddam had said, and then I would develop their line of questioning for the following day. I pointed out to him that they needed to have an Iraq expert like me when they were talking to Saddam, if only to challenge him if he seemed to be lying. I then left the room and told Bruce that if I was not involved in the actual interrogation, I would be on the next plane back to the States. He managed to calm me down and said he would talk to Bob. I was subsequently able to convince Bob that my expertise was essential to a successful debriefing.

We soon had a major change to our team. A few days after our meeting with Bob, we learned that Charlie was being replaced. This was highly unusual and another sign of trouble brewing thousands of miles away at Langley. For some reason, the pooh-bahs at HQ were uncomfortable with the way our debriefings were being conducted. Charlie heard that a replacement was coming and caught the next flight out of Baghdad. Perhaps they felt as though we weren't getting the information they needed to placate the White House quickly enough. This was typical of the way George Tenet ran things. If he didn't have a good feel for the person in charge, he asked his inner circle to find someone else. It was an ominous indication that Langley expected answers right away that would support Tenet's assurance to the president that finding WMD would be a slam dunk.

Washington consistently underestimated the difficulty of finding WMD or getting Saddam or one of his henchmen to tell us where they were. This was also true when it came to getting accurate intelligence on other matters. During the run-up to war, the CIA received intelligence that Saddam was meeting with his top aides at a leadership facility called Dora Farms on the outskirts of Baghdad. The CIA got the tip from a source supposedly close to the Iraqi dictator, and it was relayed to Langley even as Saddam was supposedly meeting with his key officials. Tenet apparently raced to the White House with the news, prompting President Bush to begin hostilities a day earlier than planned. Two F-117 Nighthawk fighters dropped four bunker-buster bombs on the complex. None of them hit the building where Saddam was supposedly holding court, but it didn't matter. He wasn't there. He wasn't even close. █████

We learned during our debriefing that Saddam was preoccupied with money. It was everything to him. Like many people who grow up poor and know deprivation and hunger from an early age, Saddam regarded money as a measure of his status and a source of his power. Money was a lot more important to him than was meeting with government officials at Dora Farms. The source had fed the United States a story that conformed to what we expected: Saddam would be attending to the affairs of state, just as any leader would before a crisis that threatened his regime. But whether it was money or writing, Saddam was more interested in things other than the humdrum business of government. With the coalition preparing to pursue him, he had delegated much of the running of the government to his top aides. Saddam's unpredictability confounded the United States right from the start of the war.

Money was also an irritant for Saddam in his relations with others. On several occasions Saddam derided individuals who he thought were stealing from him. When he did this, an expression of contempt crossed his face, as though this was the lowest thing a person could do. He described his son-in law Husayn Kamel in this way. Husayn Kamel became world-famous after he defected to Jordan in 1994 with his brother, Saddam Kamel— who was also Saddam Hussein's son-in-law—and their families. Subsequently, the Kamel brothers grew tired of living in Amman and were led to believe that they would be forgiven if they returned to Iraq. They did so in 1996, but they were denounced as traitors, ordered to divorce their wives, and killed in a firefight with Saddam's security forces. Saddam told us about Husayn's wheeling and dealing—how he often started up companies to

launder money through Jordan, ███████████████████
██
████████. Bruce told Saddam that Husayn Kamel sounded like a very untrustworthy person. Saddam responded, "Now you know why he is where he is."

I asked Saddam about the money that was found in his possession when he was captured. Saddam smirked and gave an angry snicker. He named a large dollar amount. ████████████
████████████████████ he asked. ███████████████████
"That was the amount I had with me at the time the U.S. forces arrived. Some of your people helped themselves to my money." Saddam was dead serious. You could see that he was incensed by the thought of someone stealing from him and wanted us to account for the missing money. I told him that it was unlikely that GIs would have stolen anything, given the high-profile nature of the raid and the media blitz that would follow, and further that U.S. Special Forces didn't do things like that. At this point Saddam motioned me to give him my pen and notebook and said, "May I?" I gave him my pen and notebook and he wrote out a document stating for the record that ████████████ was missing from his possession. With a great flourish he signed the note and gave me back my notebook. I had this in my notebook for a day or so, but realized that I couldn't keep the document. We had been told by the lawyers that anything he said or wrote was discoverable and therefore all documents had to be turned over for the eventual prosecution. Now I wish I had just kept it as a keepsake of our time together. Instead I handed it to one of my teammates and we sealed it in a zip-lock bag and put it in a safe. I am sure this piece of paper is in a folder in a box—somewhere.

We were severely constrained by lack of documents during our early debriefings. We didn't know about, or have access to, a huge trove of Iraqi records that was in the U.S. Army's possession. In an undertaking such as Operation Iraqi Freedom, synergy and the ability to coordinate actions among disparate elements of the invading force proved to be impossible. These documents would have been invaluable because we could have shown Saddam that we had the goods on him, cracking his wall of self-assuredness. When I found out about the archive of captured Iraqi documents two years later, I felt sick. This information would have made our debriefing, as well as the FBI's, much more fruitful. It was further proof of how unprepared the intelligence community was for Saddam's capture.

Saddam's government kept an archive of the meetings of the Revolutionary Command Council. It was the highest-ranking government decision-making body, and Saddam was its chairman. Notes from the meetings would have been extremely useful in our debriefing. In any successful debriefing, knowledge is power. You don't have to torture people or threaten them with physical harm. If you show a detainee that you can document the facts, it severely weakens his ability to withhold information. Most detainees claim to be innocent. But once you start asking questions based on solid information, the detainee becomes nervous and indecisive. You have a better chance of learning more because you have limited his ability to give false or misleading answers. Suddenly the detainee starts offering information in hopes that his cooperation will bring leniency later on.

Although he often said he looked forward to our meetings, this didn't mean he was especially cooperative. For him it was a way to pass the time. Sometimes when we were trying to get him to explain things to us, Saddam misinterpreted our questions, implying we were ignorant. Sometimes he would use several divergent threads of thought to answer a straightforward question. He would say things like, "I will tell you my point soon, but first I must tell you about X." This would then produce a long lecture about a seemingly unrelated topic. Then Saddam would zero back to the question and tie it to the topic he'd been lecturing about.

Saddam was the most suspicious man I have ever met. He was always answering questions with questions of his own, and he would frequently demand to know why we had asked about a certain topic before he would give his answer. We would ask him a question about a certain event during his presidency, and he would begin his answer by going back to the rule of Saladin. After a few such long-winded answers, Bruce stopped him and said, "Saddam, I think we need you to focus more on the immediate question and not go into so much historical detail." Saddam would then look perplexed and answer, "But what I am saying is very important, and you must hear all of it." I often wondered afterward how many people told Saddam Hussein to keep it brief and lived to tell about it.

He was not without his lighter side, though. He did have a sense of humor, which he would put on display when he felt like diverting our questions. From time to time Saddam would tell us funny anecdotes culled from his experiences leading Iraq. He told us of a time during the 1990s when he went to Lake Habbaniya for a meeting but didn't bring his usual redundant circles of security with him, instead bringing only a few bodyguards.

Soon he was enveloped by a crowd of well-wishers chanting his name. The crowd swelled as word spread that Saddam was in town, and soon his bodyguards were overwhelmed. At one point a guard threw a young boy to the ground as Saddam made his way to the waiting car. Saddam saw this, saw the boy pick up a stick, and then winked at the boy. Saddam called the guard's name, and when he turned to face Saddam, he got whacked on the side of the head with the stick—the boy's revenge for being thrown to the ground. At this point Saddam broke out in laughter. We laughed with him. I said, "Saddam, that was a very funny story." He replied, "I have another," and proceeded to tell us a few more anecdotes similar to the one recounted above. The one thing all the stories had in common was that they ended with someone experiencing physical punishment with Saddam being the instigator of the punishment.

Saddam's temper flared when we touched on sensitive areas, notably his personal behavior. One day we discussed Iraq-Syria relations, a topic that annoyed him. He nervously picked at his fingernails, a tic that showed us we had hit a nerve. On those occasions I pushed him harder to answer the question. Once he figured out where my line of questioning was going, he would frown and hold out his hand in front of everyone and pick at the dirt from under his fingernails. If we persisted, he would begin to clean his teeth.

When the conversation moved into areas that made him uncomfortable, he would claim that we were interrogating him and that the discussion was no longer about history. When I asked him about trade between Syria and Iraq, Saddam erupted: "Trade? Who cares about trade? Do you think Saddam Hussein is a tradesman? This is the scum of history." Some things Saddam wouldn't talk about at all. These tended to be about his personal security, his relations with other Arab leaders, his relations with those he deemed loyal, and intelligence matters. Saddam also told us he had only two friends in the world, but he wouldn't tell us who they were.

What made the sessions so stimulating was that we had a chance to question Saddam about things that no one had ever asked him about before. These questions both knocked Saddam off balance and kept him talking. He wanted to provide answers for the historical record and sound convincing about it. Sometimes he was clearly surprised by our questions, as when we asked about his wives (he had two: Sajida and a flight attendant from Iraqi Airways, Samira Shahbandar; he was visibly uncomfortable when talking about them). He occasionally felt he had given away too much and tried to take back things he had said. We set aside time to build rapport, but we were constrained by the fact that we didn't know how long we'd have with Saddam and there were lots of subjects that policymakers in Washington wanted us to cover. Our CIA team knew far more about Saddam and Iraq than the FBI debriefers who followed us, but we ended up getting far less time to question him. George Tenet and his cronies on the seventh floor of the CIA in Washington just didn't understand what went into a successful debriefing.

Saddam clung tenaciously to the idea that he was still head of state and referred to himself as the president. For this reason, we would not address him as Mr. President or Mr. Saddam. We would call him only by his first name. He seemed a bit put off by this at first but soon got used to it.

One day he asked a guard for something to read. The guard located a number of books in Arabic and gave them to him. Saddam devoured them. One was a book of his speeches. The next day he brought it into the interrogation room and said he wanted to read something to us. It was a speech he had given in September 1980. He told me, "Yesterday you said that it was I who started the war with Iran. I have something to say to you." He began reading the speech. It was the speech he gave justifying the invasion of Iran.

We tolerated it for a short while. We thanked Saddam for trying to educate us about the origins of the Iran-Iraq War and said we would come back to that later, but first we had other topics to discuss. I was privately disappointed. I could have listened to him talk about the war for hours. I knew that few people would ever have this opportunity. Saddam was very proud of his leadership of Iraq during the war. It was weirdly fascinating to hear him relive old battles, naturally with minor modifications to enhance his role and diminish the roles of his subordinates.

6.

The Persian Menace

--- --- ---

I asked Saddam what it was like growing up in Tikrit and how a young man from such a benighted place came to be president of Iraq. Saddam said life was difficult and his family was poor. I asked him about his relationship with his mother and his stepfather. In my years as a leadership analyst studying him, I had no reason to doubt the received wisdom that his stepfather—his father's brother, and hence his uncle too—was cruel to him and beat him as a youth. Saddam supposedly left home to escape this terror, and many of the eminent psychiatrists who later analyzed him from afar said that this was why Saddam was so confrontational and cruel, and also why he wanted nuclear weapons—a chain of logic that seemed stretched but not implausible. These views were so prevalent in the academic and intelligence communities that I found myself drawing on them in my briefings to senior policymakers.

What Saddam told me turned our assumptions upside down.

He said that he loved his stepfather very much and that he was the kindest man he knew. It was his stepfather, Saddam said, who told him to leave home, not because he was unkind but because he knew there were no opportunities in Tikrit for a youth like Saddam. For this advice Saddam remained eternally grateful. When I asked him about reports that his stepfather was abusive to him, Saddam answered: "It's not true. Ibrahim Hasan—God bless him. If he had a secret, he would entrust me with it. I was more dear to him than his son, Idham."

I thought I knew the ins and outs of the Iraqi dictator's life, but this was a revelation. It also caused me to question the diagnoses of the doctors and psychiatrists I had worked with at the CIA. We had been hearing for years that Saddam suffered from a bad back that caused him great pain. Like any man in his sixties, Saddam's back would get stiff, but he was in far better shape than our medical experts thought. I remember his driver, Samir, saying Saddam had enormous stamina and made his companions look like a bunch of whiners when they were on the run. Despite some prostate problems and high blood pressure, which was not unusual for a man his age, he was in fine health. He had some phobias, however. He constantly complained about his plywood cell, claiming he was allergic to the wood. He probably felt poorly because the prison was dark and it was winter in Iraq, a damp time of year. To be honest, we all felt a bit sick.

The medical experts at the CIA also told us that Saddam had given up red meat and cigars. Saddam laughed when I asked him if he had given up cigars. He said he didn't know where I was getting my intelligence, but it was dead wrong. Anybody who spent time with him, he continued, knew he loved cigars and smoked four every day. Saddam then playfully asked if I had any cigars. Unfortunately, I don't smoke them, I told him. Saddam seemed disappointed. He also said he ate red meat. Again I wondered about the value of medicos diagnosing people they had never met. Years later, I did some work on Kim Jong Il, and the doctors at the CIA said roughly the same things about Kim as they had said about Saddam.

In some respects, Saddam's circumstances in captivity were similar to those he experienced when he was president. He couldn't necessarily go where he wanted when he wanted. He was surrounded by guards twenty-four hours a day, seven days a week. If he wanted something, he asked for it—although in his current circumstances he was now getting "No" as an answer to most of his requests. ████████████████ ████████████████████████ He would ask his guards what time it was. He wanted to know what time of day it was because he needed to perform his daily prayers. A lot of us thought this was a power thing—that Saddam pretended to be pious so he could exert some control over his routine. Not true. One of the interesting things I learned about Saddam was that, late in life, he became religious. He was not a Wahhabist, or a jihadist. Nor was his religious motivation because of some secret alliance with al-Qaeda. I think religion just seemed more important to him in the twilight of his life. It was a very personal decision on his part. But that did not stop Saddam from trying to use religion when he wanted to thwart our interrogation. Often when we would touch on subjects that Saddam didn't want to discuss, he would begin to look around and say, "Where is the guard? I think it is time for my prayer!"

A funny thing happened one day when Saddam tried to use this tactic to fend us off. We had been speaking about WMD when he suddenly asked what time it was and said, "I think it's time for my prayer." Sure enough, ten minutes later the guard knocked on the door and said it was that time. Wanting to accommodate Saddam but also not let him feel he could dictate the timing and tempo of our debriefings, we told him we'd finish up and let him leave. As was our custom, we tried to end on a light note by talking about something nonconfrontational. Bruce began by saying that Saddam shared many comparisons with our sixteenth president, Abraham Lincoln. At this, Saddam's ears perked up. How so, he asked. Well, Bruce continued, you both were presidents during a time of war, you both came from very humble roots, and you both had limited military backgrounds but found yourself commanding armies in life-and-death struggles. Saddam found this fascinating—so much so that when the guard knocked on the door to remind him that it was prayer time, Saddam waved him off because he was more interested in what Bruce had to say. Saddam felt the polygrapher was someone who had come to his senses and understood the true worth of the man sitting before him.

During some of our first debriefings with Saddam, he could barely keep his eyes open. He would complain that he was unable to sleep because his cell was close to the front door. The arrival of new prisoners, which happened every night, kept waking him up. Watching him try to stay awake was like watching an infant who had stayed up past his bedtime. His eyelids would become heavy and he would yawn incessantly. Sometimes I thought the military disturbed his sleep intentionally. Saddam also complained about hearing loud music. After a few heavy-lidded sessions, we asked that his cell be moved. The military obliged, and Saddam started to get a full eight hours of sleep a night. When refreshed and relaxed, he was ready to do battle with his inquisitors. Saddam was also frustrated that the military would not allow him to have any paper or a pen. "I am a writer," he said to me indignantly, "and I need these things to record my thoughts! When the U.S. Army came and got me I was writing a book that is now unfinished. Why cannot I have that now? How will I hurt myself?" I knew what he was saying made some sense, but this was the military's show, and it was not going to risk Saddam's taking his own life, as exceedingly difficult and improbable as such an act would be.

During his trial, Saddam claimed he had been tortured during his captivity. Maybe he was referring to sleep deprivation, or getting roughed up during capture, or the fact that he was not allowed to write to his heart's content. I can say categorically that he was never tortured. Saddam was treated in an exemplary fashion—far better than he treated his old enemies. He got three meals a day. He was given a Koran and an Arabic translation of the Geneva Conventions. He was allowed to pray five times each day according to his Islamic faith. By contrast, when a cell of Shia rebels with ties to Iran was captured by Saddam's Mukhabarat in 1999 and taken to Abu Ghraib, they were held for three days and then tortured. The inflictions they suffered are too graphic for these pages. But I never forgot those poor souls who experienced unspeakable horror and pain before their deaths at the hands of Saddam's thugs.

At one session, when questioned about the Iranian leadership,

Saddam tried to be statesmanlike. He adopted a tone of magnanimity, although it was tinged with condescension. But he couldn't hide his hatred of the Iranians. Sometimes he became unhinged just talking about them. At one point I mentioned that the United States and Iran had many things in common. I asked him if he knew that some people called Los Angeles "Tehrangeles" because of its large Iranian population. Saddam started laughing. I said that the Iranian people had even held a candlelight vigil for the victims of 9/11. At this, Saddam got a pained look. "That is the two faces talking. Ohhh, go run to your friends the Iranians. Yes, be their friend," he said with a mocking laugh. "See how long that will last!" Saddam then said that his government expressed condolences through a public letter that he had Tariq Aziz give to Ramsey Clark, the former attorney general and a most unlikely conduit to President Bush. Saddam asked with great force and confusion, "Didn't you read Tariq Aziz's letter to Ramsey Clark? Who is more important, Tariq Aziz or the mayor of Tehran?"

Saddam truly saw himself as the guardian of the Arabs against the Persian menace. Because of this, he said, the whole world saw Iraqis as the "most noble people." Saddam then resumed his tirade against Iran. "The Iranians are untruthful. They assume that all people are liars. They will announce something and then do the opposite. That is the Iranian mentality." Later on in the session he added, "Iran is still ambitious to expand into the Arab world in the name of Islam. They think that if the time is right, they will have a leadership role in the liberation of al-Quds [Jerusalem]. When they take over, they think they will establish the Islamic realm. ██████████████

███████████████████████████ So whoever owns these weapons can say that they can liberate Jerusalem. They [Iran] think they can lead the Arab nation." Saddam also blamed the Iranians for the 1996 assassination attempt on his son Uday.

The next session was more of the same. Saddam came in his usual way, sat down and greeted us, and immediately launched into a long monologue about the Iran-Iraq War. "There were 548 acts of war committed against Iraq prior to the war," Saddam said, and then proceeded to recite all 548 to us. We asked him to discuss specific points, including the sinking of several Iraqi and foreign ships at the entrance to the Shatt al-Arab, Iraq's outlet to the Persian Gulf and the trigger for the conflict. "We sent to the UN 290 memorandums," he said. "Iran answered with one . . . The Iranian defense Minister on 22 September said that if the Iranian forces attacked Iraq, they would not stop until they reached Baghdad." In 1988, the liberation of the al-Faw Peninsula, located at the head of the Shatt al-Arab waterway, was a turning point for Iraq in the war because it drove Iranian forces from Iraqi territory once and for all.

Saddam went on for hours about Iran. It moved him to talk in ways that few other subjects did. He felt that his country had behaved gallantly during the war and that the test of arms between the two countries proved that Iraq had the "most noble fighters." When we asked him why he started the war, Saddam took issue with the premise of the question, even though military analysts generally agree that Iraq threw the first punch with one hundred thousand troops and nearly two hundred warplanes.

Saddam insisted Iran was responsible for the hostilities because it had not honored an agreement to return two settlements to Iraq, had set fire to Iraqi oil wells, and had stationed U.S.-made artillery pieces close to the Iraqi border. Iraq "repelled" the Iranian artillery, Saddam said, and he wrote the Iranian leadership three times warning against an escalation. "They continued the shelling of Basra and the oil infrastructure," Saddam charged. "In Diyalah they staged attacks from the second plot of land [called Said Saah]. We took prisoners. One we kept approximately ten years to show that the war did not start on 22 September [when Iraq launched its invasion], but for us on 4 September. The Iranians tried to assassinate members of the command. They tried to kill Tariq Aziz, Latif Nusayif Jasim, and Mudathir Badr al-Din. Even with that we were not at war. They committed over 240 aerial intrusions and airstrikes." When asked about Ayatollah Khomeini's call for the Iraqi Shia to overthrow the government, Saddam said, "Meddling in the internal affairs—that's an act of aggression."

Saddam tried to avoid commenting directly on his army's use of chemical weapons during the Iran-Iraq War, but his tight-lipped approach became increasingly difficult because he wanted us to know that Iran had used the same weapons and claimed that Iraq had used them only for defensive purposes. Saddam pointed out that Iran was the first to use chemical weapons in the September 1981 battle of Khorramshahr, the deepest Iraqi penetration into Iran and the place where it was stopped in its tracks.

When asked about Iraq's tactics during the war, Saddam curtly replied, "Go ask the MOD [Ministry of Defense]." Saddam clearly didn't want to talk about his use of missiles against

Iran and, as usual, turned the missile war between Iraq and Iran as an Iranian provocation. He said Libya gave Iran missiles to hit Iraq. "I talked to the Iranians over the radio. I said this is a losing method. We need to avoid this type of war. Up to that time, I was reluctant to use these methods [missile attacks on Iranian territory] to reach Iran. I knew this would cause other problems. When Iran wouldn't stop, a suggestion was to produce the Scud missile. When we started hitting Iran, the Iranians responded. We didn't take any action against Iran until they did something first. We returned everything in equal measure."

I switched gears and asked Saddam about the removal of President Ahmad Hasan al-Baqr, his predecessor as head of state in Iraq. I told Saddam that many analysts in the United States believed that he forced Ahmad Hasan from power so that he could take over the country. I told Saddam that I knew he was concerned about the future of Iraq because of the rise of Shia fundamentalism under Khomeini, which threatened to infect Iraq's largely powerless Shia majority, and that perhaps he thought he could provide younger, more vigorous leadership to deal with Iran. Saddam watchers also suspected that he had Ahmad Hasan killed years later when things began to go badly during the Iran-Iraq War and that Saddam may have worried he might be overthrown in a coup. As Saddam listened, I could see the anger rising in him. I couched my remarks by saying they were mostly rumors, but I wanted to hear Saddam's take on them. I'm not sure that my nuanced explanation of Western interpretations of his actions was fully conveyed in the translation. Saddam told me he had never heard such nonsense.

Saddam insisted that it was Ahmad Hasan al-Baqr's idea to

turn power over to him. He said that Ahmad Hasan was getting on in years, his health was beginning to fail, and he didn't want to be president anymore. According to Saddam, Ahmad Hasan said that Saddam was the only person who knew how the government worked and who could hold it together. Saddam claimed that at first he demurred because he "did not like authority," improbably saying that he'd wanted to go back to Tikrit and turn his hand to farming. However, he could see the threats gathering and after much soul searching decided to take Ahmed Hasan up on his offer.

At this point I asked Saddam if this was the reason he organized the infamous 1979 Ba'ath Party conference at which many members were purged and later executed. Again, I could see his anger rising. He said that one of the reasons for holding the conference was to uncover a plot against Iraqi Ba'athists by Syrian Ba'athists. He said that he found that even his secretary was part of the plot. These were treasonable activities and the party acted out of self-preservation. By then his left eye was twitching.

As usual, we wanted to end the session with a benign question, so I asked Saddam what he liked to read. He said he liked to read history and Arabic stories. I asked him his favorite book and he said *The Old Man and the Sea*, by Ernest Hemingway. "Think about it," he said. "A man, a boat, and a fishing line. These are the only ingredients to the book, but they tell us so much about man's condition. A marvelous story." We ended there, but I could tell Saddam was annoyed with me for my comments about Ahmad Hasan al-Baqr.

My suspicions were confirmed at the following session. I began to question Saddam, and he instantly put up his hand and said that he had something to say to me. "I want to talk to you about saying hurtful things. Yesterday, you said that I was responsible for the death of Ahmad Hasan al-Baqr. Did you know that he was my relative? Did you know that I loved him like a father? Did you know that we were friends?" As he continued, I saw he was again working himself up into a highly emotional state. I did not want him to use this as a pretext to shut down on us. I told him that I thought our discussion had been very fruitful. I said that he had told me things that I hadn't known before. I feigned interest about the Syrian threat to the Ba'ath Party and said I had asked about Ahmad Hasan al-Baqr only because of the rumors I had heard. Saddam looked mollified and said, "OK."

There was one humorous moment in our discussions of Iran. I deliberately said something wrong about one of his cabinet ministers in hopes of provoking Saddam to correct me and tell us more about the individual. Saddam mistook my ploy for genuine ignorance and commented that I was a man of low intelligence. At which point Bruce said, "Oh, then you think my friend here is dumb. You mean dumb like sending your entire air force for safekeeping to your worst enemy, Iran, huh?" At which point Saddam blanched for a moment and looked stunned, as if he couldn't believe anyone would dare question his judgment in such a disrespectful way. During the first Gulf War in 1991, Saddam sent planes and naval vessels to Iran so they wouldn't be destroyed. He naively thought that Iran would return them. As of the writing of this book, those planes—or whatever is left of them—have yet to make it back to Baghdad. Some have even speculated that he did this to draw Iran into his war with the United States.* Suddenly he broke into a grin, his shoulders started to shake, and he began to laugh. He held up his index finger and said, "Touché." We all cracked up.

Part of Saddam's efforts to inflate his historical importance was to put himself in the most positive light and hope that we wouldn't know enough to contradict him. Saddam told us that he did not disrespect Ayatollah Khomeini and even claimed to go out of his way to discourage undue celebration in Iraq after the Iranian leader died in June 1989. He said he received a call from one of his aides gloating about Khomeini's death and told him to show respect for the dead holy man. This stretched our credulity to the breaking point. Saddam especially hated Khomeini, whom he considered a mortal foe. I asked Saddam why, if he was so respectful of Khomeini, he referred to him in such derogatory terms in his radio speeches during the war. Saddam then asked me for specific dates and times and the words that were used. I told him that I would bring them to our next meeting if he wanted to see what I was talking about.

I then asked him about Khomeini's exile in Iraq, from 1965 to 1978. When Iraq and Iran signed the 1975 Shatt al-Arab agreement to end their border disputes, Saddam said the two countries had agreed not to meddle in each other's affairs. "Khomeini was a guest of Iraq. So when you have a guest in your country with political problems, that does not mean . . . you have bad relations with that country. So as a guest we respect his

---

*Michael Axworthy, *Revolutionary Iran: A History of the Islamic Republic* (London: Allen Lane, 2013), p. 311.

security. After the agreement, he talked to reporters and produced tapes. We sent to him an RCC [Revolutionary Command Council] member to explain to him the agreement between us and the Shah . . . We told our representative that if the ayatollah respected this, things could go on as is. If he refused to abide by this, we would end his stay. When he was told about the agreement, Khomeini said he would have to continue working against the shah." At that point Khomeini told the regime that he would leave Iraq. He first tried to go to Kuwait but was denied entry. Saddam claimed that the shah tried to pressure Saddam to keep Khomeini in Iraq, but that Saddam decided to let him go to Paris at the ayatollah's request.

Saddam never wanted anyone to think that he would do anything at the instigation of the shah. However, that didn't square with the historical record. I think Saddam did not want to appear to be doing the shah's bidding by kicking Khomeini out of Iraq. Even when he discussed the negotiations of the Shatt al-Arab treaty, which was signed nearly thirty years before our meetings, Saddam insisted that he had the upper hand when dealing with the shah and that it was the shah who was the supplicant in any peace moves. Saddam said he sent a letter to the shah saying that if Khomeini had stayed in Iraq and continued to work against the shah, both the Iranians and the Iraqis would think that Saddam's government had gone back on its word. "It's one of the reasons why the Khomeini government was so hostile to Iraq," said Saddam. "I think that anyone who reaches power in Iran will not be friendly to Iraq."

Saddam continued to ramble on about his friends and rivals within Iraq. Hard as it was to believe, Saddam told us he loved the Kurds. "I don't know what it is about them that I admire so. Maybe it is the fact that they are simple folk. I love simple country people. I get along with them better. Country people are more direct. The Kurds before 1961 were a simple people. Any valuable things in Baghdad could be entrusted to a Kurdish person with confidence. After 1961, old hostilities started in the north, and the government has to respond. Before that, they were truthful . . . But after Halabja, we got a bad name with the Kurds. The Kurds lost their faith and trust in us." What made this statement so bizarre was that Saddam said it in a mournful way, as though he couldn't quite understand why the Kurds got so upset with him. Saddam's army attacked the Kurdish city of Halabja with chemical weapons near the end of the Iran-Iraq War. Thousands died and many thousands more were injured, mostly civilians, in what was officially classified as genocide against Iraqi Kurds in retribution for their support of Iran. We learned after his fall that, ironically, Saddam had not ordered the use of chemical weapons at Halabja but had found out about it after the fact. According to Saddam, the attack on Halabja and the use of chemical weapons there were the work of General Nizar al-Khazraji, a former Iraqi army chief of staff. When Saddam found out about the attack, he was furious. Not because it was a human rights violation to attack innocent civilians, but because the attack came in a section of Iraq sympathetic to the Iranians. Saddam feared, accurately, that the Iranians would trumpet the news of chemical weapons use to focus international outrage on Baghdad.

Saddam's expressions of love for the Kurdish people did not extend to its leadership. He viewed both Masud Barzani, now president of Iraqi Kurdistan, and Jalal Talabani, who would serve as president of Iraq from 2005 until July 2014, as liars and untrustworthy politicians who had poisoned the minds of their people against Saddam. "It is very hard to trust the word of Jalal Talabani. He knows [my opinion on this] because I told it to him face-to-face: 'You take a stance at night and in the morning you take a different stance.'"

7.

Turbans in Politics

S addam held a dim view of religion in politics—particularly
when it did not suit his needs. He was especially wary of
Wahhabism, the austere form of Islamic fundamentalism with
roots in Saudi Arabia. Saddam thought that Sunni fundamentalism was a greater threat to his regime than were Iraq's majority
Shiites or even the Iranians. Saddam, like many of the region's
leaders, had risen to power at a time when Arab nationalism was
ascendant. But now it was on the wane, supplanted by Islamic
fundamentalism as the animating impulse of the region. Saddam
thought this would bring nothing but trouble. "I am convinced
from all those years since 1977—and I have written about this—
that any attempt to introduce religion into government and politics will lead to insult to religion and will damage politics, and
the [Ba'ath] Party went forward on this principle."*

---

*Debriefing notes, January 13, 2004.

Saddam believed Wahhabism would spread faster than any-one realized because it excited people who were disillusioned by the failures of Arab political leaders over the previous fifty years. He said that Iraq's borders with Jordan, Kuwait, Turkey, Saudi Arabia, and Iran made it an ideal base for fundamentalism. "Iraqi people lived this life in balance. Injecting any foreign fac-tors will make it unbalanced. So, when you bring Wahhabism to Iraq, Iraq can become unbalanced."*

Saddam had used a spoils system, handing out cars and cash to tribal sheiks to maintain the loyalty of Sunni tribes. What made the Wahhabis so threatening to him was that they came from his own Sunni base of support. They would be difficult to root out without alienating the Iraqi tribes, and they could rely on a steady stream of financial support from Saudi Arabia. If the Wahhabists were free to spread their ideology, then his power base would rot from within.

In my trailer at night, I thought about what Saddam had said about fundamentalism. Many nights I would just put on my headphones and listen to music before falling asleep. But other nights something Saddam had said would keep me awake—and this was one of those nights. In all the years I had spent analyzing Saddam, I never for a second thought he was fearful of Wahhabis or Salafists, Sunni Muslims who strictly adhere to the teachings of Muhammad in the Koran and the Hadith, a collection of Muhammad's utterances recorded by one of his companions.

To be sure, there were moments of high tension with the fundamentalists, notably in 1996 when Saddam executed one of

*Debriefing notes, January 12, 2004.

the leaders of the Dulaim, among the largest Sunni tribes in Iraq, on charges of treason. But I, along with other analysts, viewed that as a show of power by Saddam and his tribal network. We did not detect any religious overtones in the execution. We were aware of a growing fundamentalist movement in Iraq that hid from the Mukhabarat and viewed the United States with suspicion. But that was as far as it went. As analysts, we just assumed this was another faction that Saddam would crush if it became a serious threat. As I tossed and turned one night, I wondered where our analysis had come up short. How was it that the Butcher of Baghdad feared the Sunnis who formed the backbone of his support? Whether he meant to or not, Saddam was giving us clues about the man behind the myth, and some of what he said was exactly the sort of thing the White House would not want to hear. Instead of the tyrant caricature that existed of him in the West, Saddam was saying there were countervailing pressures that he had to be aware of when governing—that even he had to tread cautiously in dealing with tribal politics in the Sunni heartland.

Saddam had subjugated the majority Shiites, often through force. However, he was never able to fully eradicate the Shia threat to his regime. Wisely, he turned his weakness into strength. He used the Shia specter as a way to keep the loyalty of Sunnis who might otherwise want to topple him. Saddam had positioned himself as the protector of the Sunni minority.

But he knew he would never be trusted by Sunni fundamentalists. Wahhabist forces, according to Saddam, were trying to infiltrate the regime and threatening his grip on power. Saddam illustrated the threat by telling us about Kamel Sachet al-Janabi, a promising Iraqi general who had been a hero in the Iran-Iraq War and had served on Saddam's general staff. After Iraq's invasion of Kuwait, Kamel Sachet had been sent to Kuwait to help with the occupation. From this vantage point, he witnessed the destruction of the Iraqi army in the Gulf War in 1991. The army was the institution that he held most dear, and its degradation marked the beginning of his disillusionment with the regime.

Saddam told us he was fond of Kamel Sachet. He took the general off active duty after the Gulf War but made him part of his "warriors directorate" of officers who continued to wear their uniforms and draw a salary even though they were officially retired. During the 1990s, Kamel Sachet began to spend a lot of time on religious work. Saddam drew him aside and told him that religion was a noble cause, but to be careful about his new friends. Saddam learned that Kamel Sachet had ignored his advice and was communicating with the Wahhabis.

In late 1998, Saddam struck first before a suspected coup could take place. He had Kamel Sachet arrested and executed for plotting against the regime. The plot, if there was one, had not even gotten to its first stages. As Saddam told Kamel Sachet's story, pain was etched on his face. But loyalty was paramount. Once Saddam judged a man disloyal, his life was in jeopardy. Years later, I read a remarkable book, *The Weight of a Mustard Seed*, by Wendell Steavenson. The author uncovered the story of Kamel Sachet and his demise at the hands of the Mukhabarat. Kamel Sachet was a loyal Iraqi general who became disillusioned with Saddam's leadership after the invasion of Kuwait, Iraq's Arab neighbor. Sachet, a deeply religious man, soon gravitated to Sunni religious zealots, who were eventually accused of trying to overthrow Saddam and were executed. However, what Steavenson did not uncover was that it was Kamel Sachet's ties to Wahhabists that were his undoing. A few years later, Kamel Sachet's sons became part of the al-Qaeda in Iraq insurgency fighting the United States.

Saddam denied any connection to al-Qaeda, insisting he was a determined foe of the group. We asked him about 9/11, and he was quick to point out the fallacy of arguments that accused him of involvement. "Why do you think I did this? Look at who was involved. Who carried out the plot itself. What countries did they come from? Saudi Arabia. And this man Muhammad Atta? Was he an Iraqi? No. He was Egyptian. Why don't you go ask Hosni Mubarak about who was responsible for the attack! Why do you think I was involved in the attacks?"

I mentioned that Americans who follow the news in Iraq were outraged by Uday's editorial in his newspaper, *Babil*, in which he appeared to be gloating over the attacks. "What does it matter what my son says? Was he a member of the government? No." I explained to Saddam that *Babil* editorials carried special weight because they were coming from his onetime heir apparent and that some people in our government still thought that Uday spoke for him. Saddam just rolled his eyes and laughed when he heard this.

When it came to understanding the Iraqi street, Saddam was without parallel. No one knew better the dreams and desires of Iraqis—and the betrayals they were capable of. But when it came to understanding how nations interacted, or how a faraway country like the United States worked, Saddam was out of his depth. He never fully grasped the impact of 9/11, which he saw as something that might bring Iraq and the United States closer together. Since the terrorist attacks on New York and Washington were the work of Islamic extremists, Saddam thought the United States would need his secular government to help fight the scourge of Wahhabist militancy. In this, Saddam correctly diagnosed the ailment but was woefully wrong about the next step of treatment. The United States had decided the days of tolerating Saddam were over. It was time to overthrow him.

Saddam never accepted guilt for any of the crimes he was accused of committing, and he frequently responded to questions about human rights abuses by telling us to talk with the commander who had been on the scene. The closest he ever came to admitting a mistake was when we talked about the 1990 invasion of Kuwait. Iraq's stated reason for the invasion was that Kuwait was stealing Iraqi oil by "slant drilling," a practice whereby a country extracts oil from wells beyond its own border. Other factors included Iraq's inability to repay the $50 billion it had borrowed from Kuwait during the Iran-Iraq War and the overproduction of oil by Kuwait (and the United Arab Emirates) that busted OPEC's target price of eighteen dollars per barrel and depressed Iraq's oil revenues (Kuwait acquiesced to the OPEC standard several days before the invasion). The invasion, and Iraq's seven-month occupation, drew worldwide condemnation and precipitated the Gulf War. Some four hundred thousand Kuwaitis, roughly half the population, fled the country. Iraq looted Kuwait and, as its soldiers retreated, set fire to six hundred of its seven hundred oil wells, damaging the environment and causing health problems for Kuwaitis.

At our first meeting, I had noticed that Saddam seemed to flinch when Kuwait was mentioned. When I next brought it up, his face took on an anguished look, and he tried to change the subject. I decided to let it go because we were trying to get him talking, and I didn't want him to shut down before we got a conversation started. During our following meeting I brought up Kuwait again. Saddam put both hands on his head and said, "Uggghhhhh, this gives me such a headache!" It was as direct an acknowledgment as we were going to get that the invasion was a mistake that he was never able to live down.

In 1990, the thirty-four-nation coalition against Iraq fielded 700,000 troops, 540,000 of them American, most of whom were initially deployed to Saudi Arabia. (The Saudis covered $36 billion of the war's overall cost of $60 billion.) We asked Saddam if he'd ever considered using WMD preemptively against U.S. troops in Saudi Arabia. "If your troops had concentrated in any other country than Saudi Arabia," he said, "we would have attacked them. Saudi Arabia is holy land for us, and for you to be there was a sin. We did not want to commit a sin by attacking you there. No, we never thought about using weapons of mass destruction. It was not discussed . . . Use chemical weapons against the world? Is there anyone with full faculties who would do this? Use these weapons when they had not been used against us?"

Saddam was asked about his intentions in October 1994, when Iraq moved ten thousand troops, including elements of two elite Republican Guard divisions, toward the Kuwait border. He said the movements were just exercises designed to keep the United States and Kuwait guessing about his intentions and to familiarize his forces with potential battlefields in southern Iraq. "You know we were still at war at that time since 1991," Saddam said. "So to keep the military in one place is not a good thing because the enemy will know where our troops are. So to move and maneuver them will keep the enemy wondering what was going on. We were hoping to scare the Kuwaitis into stopping the border clashes. It was mainly a scare tactic, so they were afraid. Some people were even leaving Kuwait because they were so scared, and that was good too, but it wasn't our intention." President Clinton, declaring it would be a "grave mistake" if Saddam thought U.S. resolve had weakened since the Gulf War, ordered American warships to the Persian Gulf and prepared a deployment of thirty-four thousand ground troops to the region. The UN Security Council also expressed strong concern about the movement of Iraqi troops, which were quickly pulled back.

The British historian and diplomat Sir Bernard Pares wrote that the Russian Revolution began in Tsar Nicholas's nursery. He was referring to the hemophiliac Tsarevich Alexis and the role his health played in the fall of the Romanov family. For Saddam, a great source of strain in his own rule occurred in the bedroom and living room of his family. This was a topic that Saddam was at times loath to talk about, yet he also took pains to make sure we understood that he was the undisputed head of his clan. When I asked him about his wife Sajida, Saddam said that it was love at first sight. He had lived with her family and had been raised from adolescence by her father, who was also his uncle, Khayrallah Tilfah. He was a Baghdad politician who had ties to military figures and who had been imprisoned by the British during World War II for having pro-Nazi sympathies. Saddam expressed great respect for Khayrallah. He also knew that by marrying his daughter he could advance his political career. Saddam failed to mention some of Khayrallah's lesser attributes. During the early part of Saddam's reign, when Khayrallah Tilfah served as mayor of Baghdad, his appetite for corruption was so ravenous that Saddam eventually had to remove him. Khayrallah would go on to write a short book, revealingly titled *Persians, Flies, and Jews: Three Whom God Should Not Have Created.*

Saddam would not discuss his wife beyond expressing his devotion to her. I asked him where she had gone. He said, "I am not telling you." When I then asked him about Samira Shahbandar, his second wife, he became annoyed. Saddam had caused a severe rift in his family by taking a second wife, which is allowed in the Islamic religion. Saddam preferred the company of Samira to his "official" wife, Sajida, the first lady of the Iraqi republic. Sajida was deeply hurt. She had turned a blind eye to his serial womanizing, but this was something she couldn't ignore. It led to bad blood between Saddam and his Tilfah relations, who had made his political ascendancy possible. "I am not going to talk about them," he told us. "We have a saying in Arabic: 'The women are separate.' We do not discuss them, and they have nothing to do with politics." It had also angered Saddam's son Uday, who was very close to his mother and disliked anyone or anything that hurt her. (Uday murdered Saddam's valet Kamel Hana in the late 1980s. Some have conjectured that Uday was upset because Hana procured women for Saddam to sleep with.)

We told Saddam that we were sympathetic, but that we had to ask these questions. I reminded him that Samira's son from her first husband had been a pilot in training in the United States in the 1990s. When the news media found out about this connection, journalists immediately began to speculate that perhaps this was a missing link in the 9/11 attacks. I explained that we knew Samira had been a stewardess and her former husband had been the head of Iraqi Airways, and that it was a natural progression in Middle Eastern families for the eldest son to go into the trade of his father. Saddam said that was true. I asked him about rumors that he had fathered a son with Samira named Ali. Saddam now had a really pained expression and seemed more annoyed than ever. "If I told you yes, would you kill him like you killed Uday and Qusay?" he asked. I looked at the Iraqi dictator and told him that I never killed anyone. We stopped for an awkward moment and stared at each other. I continued to press the question. Finally Saddam said, "In Arab culture we have a saying: 'Those who have children we regard as married, whether they have performed the ceremony or not. Those who do not have children, we regard as unmarried.' That is all I have to say." We interpreted this as confirmation that he and Samira did indeed have a son named Ali. This may not seem a very significant detail today, but for someone who followed Saddam for years, it was gratifying to finally learn that the rumors were true. Samira Shahbandar apparently did as much as she could to protect her son from the vicissitudes of Iraqi politics. She had to be aware that there were possibly remnants of the Ba'ath Party who, in desperation, might have someday reached out to Ali to carry on his father's work. Or there could be any number of Shia groups who would want to wipe out Saddam's last male heir. However, like his mother, Ali appears to have slipped away from history's grasp. That is probably fortunate for them both.

Saddam told me was proud of Uday and Qusay, but realistic about their shortcomings. He sometimes found it necessary to punish them. Uday was a particular problem for him. He said he was incensed when he learned that Uday kept a fleet of Bentleys, Jaguars, and Mercedeses in a garage in Baghdad that was protected by Republican Guard soldiers. "What kind of message are we sending to the Iraqi people, who must suffer under sanctions and do without?" So Saddam had the cars torched. The torching of the cars occurred shortly after Uday provoked the 1995 defection of Husayn Kamel, Saddam's son-in-law and second cousin, who was minister of industry and military industrialization. Uday, drunk and out of control, had gone to the Kamel residence, where a party was being held, and had gotten into a fistfight with Saddam Kamel, Husayn's brother. Saddam Kamel bested Uday in fisticuffs, which then led Uday to grab a gun and, because he was severely inebriated, shoot up the Kamel residence. Uday wounded his father's half brother Watban, who happened to get in the way. It was after this altercation that Husayn and Saddam Kamel took their wives—Saddam's daughters—and defected to Jordan. The defection of the Kamel brothers, with Saddam's daughters and grandchildren, rocked the regime and cracked the unity of Saddam's inner circle for all the world to see.

The only time that Saddam ever showed any emotion during the time I talked to him was when we discussed his daughters, Rana and Raghid. His eyes became watery and his voice quivered momentarily. He would say only, "I miss them terribly. I enjoyed a wonderful relationship with them. They loved me very much, and I loved them very much." As for their husbands, Saddam took a dark view of people he suspected of disloyalty or stealing money from him, and by his reckoning the Kamel brothers were guilty on both counts. ████████████

███████████████████████████████████

███████████████████████████████████

███████████████████████████████████

███████████████████████████████████

After their defection, Saddam said that he only wanted to get back his daughters and grandchildren. He was fearful of what might befall them in a foreign country where he could not protect them. Saddam said he did not authorize the killing of the Kamels when they returned to Iraq in 1996 and heard about it only after the fact. He said that he had just signed the document authorizing their return when he heard of the shootout that resulted in their deaths. In typical Saddam fashion, he said he picked up his pen and wrote on the decree, "The sword of justice has punished the wicked."

I asked Saddam how he had learned that Uday and Qusay had been killed. He said he had heard about their deaths on

BBC Radio. How did it make him feel that his sons were dead? Saddam said that if they had to die, this was the way he wanted them to go. "They died fighting to liberate their country. That is the noblest end that one can ask for." Saddam said they were killed not because they were his sons, but because they were Iraqis. He said that a leader who was more concerned for his children than for his people could not be respected. Saddam knew they were traveling together at the time of their deaths, but denied telling them to do so. He said they were betrayed, as he was, and he portrayed them as martyrs. I asked if he and his sons had started their flight from Baghdad together. Saddam replied, "Maybe."

██
██
██
██
██
██
██
██
█████████████████████ Uday and Qusay had holed up in Mosul in the palace of a sheik, a distant relative who was honor-bound to give them refuge. After a few weeks, the sheik became nervous because the 101st Airborne Division was patrolling near his home. He asked Saddam's sons when they might be leaving. Qusay apparently told him that they would be the judge of that and that the sheik should keep his mouth shut because they had paid him handsomely for refuge. At that point,

the sheik left Uday and Qusay at home, where they had been playing video games for weeks, ███████████████████

███

███

███

████████████████████. U.S. forces surrounded the home and a shootout ensued. Uday and Qusay were killed, ██████████

██████████████ and a bodyguard. ████████████████

███

███████████████████████████████

Saddam's relations with his own half brothers Watban, Sabawi, and Barzan were, at times, comical. It was almost as if they were an Iraqi version of the Marx brothers, with Saddam as Zeppo, the straight man, and Watban, Sabawi, and Barzan as Chico, Harpo, and Groucho. ████████████████████

███

███

███████████████████████████

Saddam told us how one day word reached him that Watban's motorcade had been driving through Baghdad, and the president's half brother had become impatient with the traffic light. Watban got out of his government car, drew his revolver, shot out the light, and went on his way. Saddam summoned Watban to the palace for a meeting. Saddam said to Watban that he had heard of an accident and asked if this was true. Saddam seemed to enjoy telling us about Watban's extreme discomfort when rehashing the details. Watban also admitted that his car had hit a pedestrian. Saddam said that he could not have this kind of activity in his country. This was a republic where the people ruled. So he sentenced Watban to direct traffic for two months in the traffic circle in Baghdad where the incident took place. Saddam guffawed at his half brother's displeasure but maintained his "I showed him who was boss" demeanor throughout the retelling of the anecdote. To Saddam, his relatives were a bit of a nuisance, to be tolerated but always reminded of their subordinate status.

His brother-in-law Adnan Khayrallah, the former minister of defense, died in a mysterious helicopter accident in 1989. Many Iraq experts speculated that Saddam had him killed because he was becoming too popular with the military and might challenge Saddam for leadership after the end of the Iran-Iraq War. Saddam insisted that he loved Adnan Khayrallah, and his affection seemed genuine when he talked about him. Saddam went to the front with Adnan Khayrallah during the Iran-Iraq War and seemed to put great store in his advice. He described losing his brother-in-law this way: "It was like a spike in my heart. That was when all the troubles started," Saddam said mournfully. I asked him what he meant, but he would not elaborate. I interpreted Saddam's remark about the troubles as a turning point in his own mind, when his reach began to exceed his grasp in regional politics, when the men he trusted to help him navigate Iraq's way in a dangerous region were becoming fewer and fewer. I could tell that Adnan Khayrallah was one of the few people Saddam trusted. Adnan Khayrallah apparently was able to sense the president's mood and make suggestions without offending him. Saddam said that there were so few people a leader could trust, one of the heaviest burdens of leadership was to make decisions alone and be sure you had people who could faithfully execute those decisions. Adnan Khayrallah was that person for Saddam.

Saddam told us the pivotal moment in his life came when he was very young: "I was the second of my brothers and sisters. The eldest, Anwar—Allah took him after four or six months. Then I was born. My father passed away before I was six months in my mother's stomach. When my father died, my mother moved into her father's [Tilfah Muslit's] house. My uncle was Khayrallah Tilfah. He was a farmer and owned land on the other side of the Tigris. He lived in Tikrit and had two or three farmers who worked for him. As is customary when a man dies, the uncles take over for the family. I had three uncles from my father's side. They were very dear and did not take me from my grandfather. Then my grandfather passed away. My uncle decided to move the family to Baghdad. I was two years old. A little time after that, a person, an uncle, came to ask for my mother in marriage. This was Ibrahim Hasan. We moved to Tikrit and then to Awja. And I entered school by my decision, not my uncle's!"

I asked Saddam if Adnan Khayrallah was influential in this decision. "No, Adnan was younger than I am. But my mother's cousin [Umar Muslit] was approximately the same age. I was about nine or ten. We were swimming in the river. It was cold and we went to the sand to get warm. He started writing numbers and letters in the sand. I said, 'What is this?' He said, '*Alif, ba, ta, tha.*' I said, 'How did you learn this?' He said, 'In school.' I said, 'Did you have to pay any money?' He said, 'No. It is free.' I said, 'Will they accept me?' He said yes. I told my uncle and my mother. My uncle said forget about school. Let's live like our fathers. We have work to do. But I decided to go to school in spite of him. My mother's cousin took me to Tikrit to register . . . My uncles on my father's and mother's sides really loved me and treated me as older than my age."

8.

Death to Shiites and Zionists

During the second week of our debriefing we began to discuss regional politics, and although Saddam tried to take the high road and not speak ill of other leaders, sometimes he could not help himself. Saddam did not have a high regard for his fellow Arab leaders. He saw himself as the greatest of the great, head and shoulders above his counterparts in the region. Though he was proud to be a leader of Arabs, he said he didn't necessarily want to lead all Arabs. "I only want to lead Iraqis," he said. "They are the noblest of all people." He saw the late King Hussein of Jordan as a man of dubious reliability and a lackey to Israel and the United States. He had nothing but contempt for the younger generation coming to power, notably Bashir al-Assad in Syria and King Abdullah in Jordan. We asked him about Egypt's Gamil Abd al-Nasir, the renowned pan-Arabist. Saddam smirked and said, "He was a good man. But he did not live long enough to see his plans through, and he was too quick to make a deal with enemies who would never keep their end of the bargain." In our conversations, Saddam never singled out another Arab leader for unqualified praise. To him, they were lesser men who had neither his intelligence nor resourcefulness.

A constant refrain in our debriefings was Saddam's complaints about his imprisonment and his requests for luxury items. He often railed about his lack of writing materials. "You must understand, I am a writer. And what you are doing by depriving me of pen and paper amounts to human rights abuse!" Saddam would also constantly request reading material to pass the time. He told us one of the guards had given him the CliffsNotes for the Arabic version of Fyodor Dostoyevsky's *Crime and Punishment*. "This man Dostoyevsky has a remarkable insight into the human condition," Saddam said. He was also a big fan of the Egyptian novelist Naguib Mahfouz and requested that we purchase for him the Arabic text of his *Cairo Trilogy*. ▮▮▮▮

▮▮▮▮▮▮▮▮▮▮▮▮▮▮▮▮▮▮▮▮▮▮▮▮▮▮▮▮▮▮▮▮
▮▮▮▮▮▮▮▮▮▮▮▮▮▮▮▮▮▮▮▮▮▮▮▮▮▮▮▮▮▮▮▮
▮▮▮▮▮▮▮▮▮▮▮▮▮▮▮▮▮▮▮▮▮▮▮▮▮▮▮▮▮▮▮▮
▮▮▮▮▮▮▮▮▮▮▮▮▮▮▮▮▮▮▮▮▮▮▮▮▮▮▮▮▮▮▮▮
▮▮▮▮▮▮▮▮▮▮▮▮▮▮▮▮▮▮▮▮▮▮▮▮▮▮
▮▮▮▮▮▮▮▮▮▮▮▮▮▮▮▮▮▮▮▮▮▮▮▮▮▮▮▮▮▮

▮▮▮▮ We often heard the muffled sounds of bombs set off by the insurgency in the distance. Saddam could clearly infer that things were not going well for the U.S.-led coalition, and he took some pleasure in our struggle to bring stability to his country. It had taken him years to achieve the level of control that he had, and the United States was badly misguided to think it could simply walk in and take his place. The idea that the Iraq invasion would be a "cakewalk"—in the immortal words of Kenneth Adelman, a former Reagan administration official and an admirer of Dick Cheney—was born of breathtaking stupidity and arrogance. Somehow the CIA and other government agencies were never able to impress on policymakers that Saddam was a savvy leader. Instead, some intelligence analysts labeled his country the "Republic of Fear," after the title of the 1989 book by Kanan Makiya, an Iraqi-born professor at Brandeis University who was a proponent of the U.S. invasion and a founder of the Iraq Memory Foundation, a nongovernmental organization dedicated to documenting the crimes of Saddam Hussein.

In truth, Saddam did not rule just by fear. He had many admirers, and he was able to win the support of influential Sunnis—and even some Shiites and Kurds. He knew his countrymen far better than we ever did or could. As the Bush administration demanded more intelligence about Iraq, and more new analysts began to work on Iraq, it became harder and harder to convey a nuanced understanding of Saddam and his intentions. More and more the Agency was overloaded with requests for information from the Bush administration. Before long it became an exercise in dumbing down, with the intelligence community providing material geared to the level of understanding of administration officials who knew little about the region. It was inevitable that the quality of analysis would suffer under such a crushing workload. Saddam was dumbfounded that the United States, with all its might and money, could be so ignorant of the Arab world.

"You are going to fail," Saddam said. "You are going to find that it is not so easy to govern Iraq." Saddam's prediction proved prescient, but in December 2003 I was curious why he felt that way. "You are going to fail in Iraq because you do not know the language, the history, and you do not understand the Arab mind." Saddam said you could not understand Iraq without understanding its geography and weather. He said that spring was his favorite season, and that it was much too short for his liking. Generally speaking, he said, Baghdadis like the fall, which lasts about two months. The Baghdad spring runs only about twenty days. "It's hard to know the Iraqi people without knowing its weather and its history. The difference is between night and day and winter and summer. That's why they say the Iraqis are hard-headed—because of the summer heat." Then Saddam gave a small chuckle and added, "Next summer, when it is hot, they might revolt against you. The summer of 1958 got a little hot. In the 1960s, when it was hot, we had a revolution. You might put that in parentheses for President Bush!"

The internal Shia threat was something that Saddam found all-consuming in the late 1990s. He once said to us, "Night and day, they will scheme against you if you let them. So you must keep a watchful eye on them." This was certainly the case after the assassination of the eminent Shia cleric Muhammad Sadiq al-Sadr, who was gunned down in 1999 while driving home from Friday prayers with his two eldest sons. In the aftermath, the regime faced its most critical test since the failed uprising in southern Iraq in 1991 following the Gulf War. For the first and only time, Saddam partly deployed his infamous Baghdad Security

Plan, a series of concentric circles in the capital with key spots manned by regime stalwarts from the Special Republican Guard.

The uprising that occurred after Muhammad Sadiq al-Sadr's assassination flared briefly inside Iraq but was put down brutally in a relatively short period of time, lasting perhaps a few weeks at best. However, in hindsight, the death of Sadr marked the beginning of the end of Saddam's regime. The Shia had been forced to witness the execution of Muhammad Baqr al-Sadr in 1980 and were largely powerless to do anything against the regime. But by 1999, Saddam's regime and its system of repression was still fearsome, though showing signs of wear and tear. Suddenly Shia groups began targeting regime officials again, shooting up Ba'ath Party offices at night and causing other acts of mayhem. When I spoke with a Sadrist in 2008 about the period after the assassination of Muhammad Sadiq al-Sadr, he said, "We no longer could just sit and accept what the regime was doing as our lot. We felt we had to do something."

Why did the Shia feel this way? Muhammad Sadiq al-Sadr was the first high-ranking Shia cleric who seemed to care for the poor and destitute in Iraq. Unlike the quietest clergy (clerics who believe that religion must be kept out of politics), led by Grand Ayatollah Ali Sistani, Sadr wanted the Shia to demand their rights and engage politically against Saddam's regime. Sadr espoused the "vocal *hawza*" (this referred to the Shia seminary in Najaf, the leading Shia religious institution in the world; Sadr felt that the needs of the people could be obtained through politics), by which the Shia would show the regime that their numbers could not be ignored—ultimately leading to the creation of an Islamic Republic in Iraq. Sadr used the money he collected in donations to create support networks for his followers. When he preached, he often spoke in the vernacular of his congregation, eschewing the more flowery and sophisticated pronouncements from other senior Shia clerics. Such acts endeared him to the millions of followers who felt that here was a cleric who was also concerned with life on earth, and not just the afterlife in heaven.

The crackdown on the Shia was brutal. Large numbers of Shiites were rounded up, tortured, and imprisoned. Muhammad Sadiq al-Sadr's eldest surviving son, Muqtada, was forced to go underground to avoid Saddam's armed thugs. Saddam responded sharply when we asked about Muhammad Sadiq: "When you tell me who killed Muhammad Baqr al-Hakim [the head of the Supreme Council of the Islamic Revolution in Iraq, a Shia op- position party, who was killed in August 2003], I will tell you who killed Sadr." Saddam actually made it seem as though he had been concerned about Hakim, which was ridiculous because the two men were sworn enemies.

When I asked again in the same meeting about Muhammad Sadiq al-Sadr, Saddam feigned ignorance. "Who?" he said, as though he could not recall the name. I repeated it and Saddam said, "That name is not familiar. Is he an Iraqi? Why don't you tell me more about him and then maybe I can remember." He knew exactly who I was talking about but did not want to say anything until I told him what I knew. Saddam played this game often during our conversations. He would feign ignorance and ask me to refresh his memory. That way he could find out what we knew. "Is this an old man or a young man?" Saddam asked. I told him that we were speaking about an old man. Suddenly the light went on in Saddam's eyes and he said, "Oh, yes. I now remember who you are talking about. Yes, members of my government did talk to this man and told him to desist from rabble-rousing. The next thing I knew he had been murdered. I ordered a special inquiry into the incident and received a report from the Mukhabarat saying that the death was the result of an internal *hawza* dispute among the senior leaders." Saddam insisted he had nothing to do with the assassination.

In effect, Saddam was saying that Muhammad Sadiq al-Sadr was killed by a fellow Shiite, Grand Ayatollah Ali Sistani, which at the time I thought was ridiculous. "[Iraq's] Shia are the ones who fought against Iran," he said. "They were part of the victory. We didn't need Sunnis to go and fight. So the Shia fought. The government does not support religion. Sadr came to meet me after the 1991 Shia uprising and betrayal. Sadr was not on top at the time. All of them were looking to normalize relations [with the regime] and saying, 'We don't intend to stir things up.' Iran likes it when the clergy act up. Since the time of the shah's father, Iran thinks if you can influence the clergy, you can influence the politics of Iraq. The Shia leader, Sadr, came to see me about his son [Saddam was most likely referring to one of Muqtada al-Sadr's elder brothers]. The information we got was that he supported the Iranian insurgents when they came into Najaf"—after Hakim was killed. Sadiq al-Sadr, Saddam continued, "said this didn't happen. He begged for my forgiveness. I granted it to him. They were warned not to use their religious authority for political ends. As citizens they can elect, vote, stand for office. They cannot wear the religious turban and enter into the political arena."

Sadiq al-Sadr had been complicit with the regime in 1991. He condemned the Shia uprising after the Gulf War and had been amply rewarded for his efforts by Saddam, who made him the chief of religious endowments. But Sadr used that perch, and the significant sums he collected, to build his ministry to the poor and champion the rights of Shiites. It was this work that eventually led him to speak out against the regime's treatment of Shiites. When I asked Saddam about the death of Sadr, he said the elder had been visited repeatedly by government envoys who told him to stop preaching against the regime. The last visit came from a member of the Special Security Organization. He told Sadr he would be killed in one month if he did not stop. ███████████████ Tariq Aziz, one of Saddam's closest advisers, was in charge of this operation, probably because he was a Christian. Sadiq al-Sadr began to wear a white shroud, a symbol to his followers that he was preparing himself for martyrdom. An intelligence operative named Tahir Jalil Habbush was ordered to carry out the assassination, and he did so with great efficiency. ██████████████████ Habbush's successful silencing of Sadr was thought to be the reason why Saddam appointed him head of the Iraqi Intelligence Service. He was the jack of diamonds in the deck of the most-wanted Iraqis, and he remains at large today.

When I asked Saddam why in 1980 he had killed Muhammad Baqr al-Sadr (cousin of Sadiq and father-in-law of Muqtada), Saddam knew exactly who I was talking about. Even so he was annoyed by the question; Saddam became distressed by questions about human rights abuses. "You Americans are going to find that it is not so easy governing Iraq," Saddam said. He then went on a long ramble about the need to separate church and state. He said that Muhammad Baqr al-Sadr had been in secret contact with Khomeini, that the Mukhabarat had listened in on their conversations, and they were planning an Islamic revolution in Iraq. Saddam said he'd told Sadr that he was free to practice his religion but had to stay out of politics. When Sadr disobeyed this command, Saddam had him arrested and executed (along with his sister, Bint al-Huda) for treasonous activities.

The topic of Saddam's weapons of mass destruction had gone from a top-tier U.S. national security threat to what was widely regarded as a wild goose chase. For years before the war, the CIA had been repeatedly asked for assessments of Saddam's WMD programs. More government man-hours, conferences, briefings, and papers were devoted to this topic than probably any other in the history of U.S. intelligence.

We tried to open up a discussion with Saddam about WMD by talking about the Iran-Iraq War. Saddam clearly saw where our questions were headed and quickly cut us off. "We're returning to a subject that has already been answered. Don't waste your time. There are more dangerous things than what you are looking for." I knew that Saddam liked to talk about Israel, and he commented on the al-Hussein missile strikes on Israel during the 1991 Gulf War. Saddam explained the political background to the strikes: "We think—not only Iraqis but all Arabs—the source of the harm, the bad things that come to us from America, it is not the confrontation between the Arabic mind and the

American mind, but is caused by Israeli pressure and Zionist lobbying in the U.S. and in the presidential elections and in supporting certain programs in America. Therefore, we think it is because of the Zionist working and lobbying in America, and this is why America is aggressive against us . . . We saw that if we attacked Israel, it might pressure the U.S. to stop attacking us. I took this decision [to fire Scuds at Israel] without consulting the command. We said before the war, if America attacks us, we will attack Israel . . . I told my commanders to hit Israeli military targets." But the Iraqis either didn't know the locations of key Israeli military sites, or, what is more likely, they just fired their missiles blindly toward Israel in the hope they might hit something.

I found it fascinating to learn that so much of what Saddam did was improvisational. This went against the grain of what analysts in Washington thought about Saddam's regime. Often in Iraq, there wasn't enough discussion of the pros and cons of a particular course of action, or intelligence collection and analysis, or debates in secret high-level councils. And when things finally went sour, there were no plans to clean up the mess. In hindsight, we probably should have had a better appreciation of Saddam's ability to ad lib. After all, we learned during the Gulf War that he would stay at a different house every night, usually one that was owned by an average citizen. Saddam would just show up and ask the homeowner if it was all right if he stayed there for the evening.

When asked why Iraq had not fully implemented Security Council resolutions after its invasion of Kuwait, Saddam responded, "Where did Iraq disagree with the UN resolutions?

The only resolution we did not agree to immediately was 661 [which imposed sanctions on Iraq]. All the rest we agreed to. But Iraq had an opinion about how these resolutions should be implemented. How many resolutions have there been about Israel? How many did they implement? But there was no war against them. Which country did not implement UN Security Council resolutions and was attacked? I can think of only one—Iraq. So Americans need to find out why America attacked Iraq. Iraq is not a terrorist nation, did not have a relationship with bin Laden, and did not have weapons of mass destruction . . . and was not a threat to its neighbors. But the American president [George W. Bush] said Iraq wanted to attack his daddy [George H. W. Bush], and 'weapons of mass destruction.'" (It wasn't just Bush who thought Iraq planned to kill his father. President Clinton fired twenty-three cruise missiles at the Iraqi Intelligence Service headquarters after receiving "compelling" evidence of a plot to assassinate the former president.) Saddam flatly denied there had been a plot to assassinate George H. W. Bush after he lost reelection in 1992 and traveled to Kuwait in early 1993. After Bush left office, Saddam said he no longer viewed him as an adversary. Saddam never understood that the purported plot was one of the primary reasons that George W. Bush wanted to oust him.

Saddam turned philosophical when asked how America got it so wrong about weapons of mass destruction. "The spirit of listening and understanding was not there . . . I don't exclude myself from this blame." This was a rare acknowledgment from Saddam that he could have done more to create a clearer picture of Iraq's intentions regarding WMD.

He said that he didn't follow the workings of the inspection teams in great detail but assigned Tariq Aziz to handle these matters. In 1991, as required by UN Security Council Resolution 687, Iraq said it had unilaterally destroyed its chemical weapons. Even though the Iraqi government ordered cooperation with the UN, local officials were not used to outsiders meddling in their business and didn't want to show the UN inspectors their files. "During war," Saddam said, "the files will be moved to protect them from airstrikes and such. So almost all government files were moved on all levels. All these actions were misconstrued as concealment or ill-intentioned." Saddam said that Rolf Ekéus, a Swedish diplomat who led the UN disarmament effort in Iraq after the Gulf War, reported "in 1995 that 95 percent of Iraq's weapons were destroyed. So from 1995 to now 5 percent has not been found and the U.S. Army is here and it is still not found."

We pointed out that for years Iraqi officials said they had no records of their weapons programs but in 1995 handed over 120 boxes of documents related to their biological arsenal. These turned up after Husayn Kamel, Saddam's son-in-law, defected to Jordan, and Iraqi officials led UN inspectors to his chicken farm, where the documents were stored. "If we had ill intentions, we would have burned it or left it hidden," Saddam said. "We didn't have any intention to resume our programs . . . even though I heard from Tariq Aziz that these documents weren't very important. Tariq Aziz didn't know why Husayn Kamel had these documents." (The Iraqis often stored sensitive materials at the homes of high officials to keep them out of the hands of international authorities.)

Not long afterward, after asserting for years that it had had only a small defensive program, Iraq admitted it had a large biological weapons arsenal. Saddam said these programs were accounted for when he provided an inventory of the weapons in Iraq to the UN. After the Gulf War, Saddam temporarily lost control of fourteen of Iraq's eighteen provinces during the Shia uprising. Ba'ath Party offices were attacked and documents were burned. "There was not one document left. They were all burned. Even property and real estate records . . . It was really great that we found some documents [about WMD] to show you. Just as Tariq said, getting 95 percent of an exam is very good." But instead of lifting the embargo, Saddam said, inspectors kept looking for the remaining 5 percent. "We were really misunderstood in an oppressive way. I don't think any other nation was oppressed and misunderstood like Iraq."

In his final years, Saddam appeared to be as clueless about what was happening inside Iraq as his British and American enemies were. His detachment from governing had led him into a trap that he couldn't escape when the 2003 invasion was imminent. He was inattentive to what his government was doing and had no real plan to prepare for the defense of Iraq. Saddam thought that, somehow, things would work out in the end, as they usually had in the past. The Americans would come, destroy parts of his country, and then would possibly get bogged down or be persuaded to stop by the international community that wished to see the violence and killing stopped. Or they would get bogged down and leave. Or the United Nations would step in and enforce a cease-fire. He did not receive detailed daily intelligence briefings and could not comprehend the immensity of the approaching storm—even his sons, Uday and Qusay, were taken by surprise at the U.S.-led attack. All his ministers looked to Saddam to have the answer. Everyone thought Saddam had a plan to deal with the coalition once it arrived in Iraq. What everyone soon learned was that there was no plan.

That was just the point: Saddam's plan to defend against coalition forces was not to have a plan. He said: "What was our choice? There were two things that would happen. Either the U.S. Army would be met with resistance or they would not. For men's honor—military honor—[and] for national honor and principles, men should fight. They should fight for their principles and, thanks to Allah, we fought and did not surrender. This was honorable . . . When the threat is broadcast and is well known, the plan is very simple. Of course it was very clear that we could not defend with the same intensity in all places . . . For the citizen, every inch of soil is dear. But for the government official, there are priorities, and they have to distribute resources according to these priorities . . . You thought that Tikrit as the home of Saddam Hussein would be given a lot of resources. But you were wrong—they went to Mosul, Kirkuk, Basra, et cetera." This was neither ignorance nor madness, but a sort of fatalism that settled in on the Iraqi leader.

Despite the importance of Baghdad, plans for its defense were haphazard. Saddam had deep respect for the military but only a primitive understanding of military affairs. He seemed to have learned little from Iraq's eight-year war with Iran. As he explained it, the Republican Guard divisions were entrenched and had to retreat to new positions to defend Baghdad, but there was not enough time to redeploy. He also had to contend with the coalition's air superiority. According to Saddam, "The purpose of the land force is that they complete the victory which is already accomplished by the air force. If we fought army against army, we would have won, not because we are better than the U.S., U.K., or France. It is a law of nature that the person who will fight for his home will fight better."

Even with limited communications, Saddam said he was aware of the multipronged nature of the U.S.-led invasion, with troops coming from the south through Kuwait, from the west through Saudi Arabia and Jordan, and from the north through Kurdish territory. When asked about his commanders, Saddam said, "They were all good. Even Rommel was a good commander but lost a battle. I think they put up a good fight. Some were able to carry out their plans and some were not. All performed their best, but this is not the nature of wars." When asked if Iraq had plans to destroy the dams on the Tigris or the Euphrates, Saddam replied dismissively, "Do you think people will destroy their own property? This is imagination. This is not practical. There was no plan to destroy the bridges because if you do, you cut up the country. In 1991 our experience was bad." During the Gulf War, many of the bridges and roads around Baghdad were destroyed or badly damaged during the U.S. aerial bombardment. This made it very difficult afterward for Saddam to control the various Iraqi governorates that had Kurdish or Shia majorities.

When we discussed the 2003 war, Saddam seemed out of touch with military realities. Many of his comments verged on the bizarre. He seemed unfamiliar with the details of the coalition offensive and the Iraqi defense. His comments about the use of U.S. air assets showed a lack of understanding of how American military doctrine integrated the actions of air and land units, and his tone suggested that he thought U.S. tactics were somehow unequal, unfair, and dishonorable.

Saddam was shown a map of Iraq to help discuss where military action had occurred, but he was unable to recall troop movements or significant actions by his ground forces. At another time, Saddam made a comparison between the Iraq War and the American Civil War, explaining that the reason the South lost to the North was that the Confederates had to fight going uphill. I could not understand what he meant and asked him to clarify. He pointed to a map and said that because the South was below the North, it meant the Southerners were always fighting a foe that was literally above them.

Saddam was asked about his 1995 decision to accept the UN Oil-for-Food Program after rejecting it for six years. The program let Iraq sell oil in exchange for medicine, food, and other humanitarian necessities. Saddam complained that the program was an affront to not only to him but also every Iraqi. He said, "What are we? Just chickens kept in the chicken coop, and if we get sick, we are to be given medicine?" Then Saddam got his nationalist dander up: "We are a nation with an army, and schools, and universities, and colleges. We understood that most of the oil goes to America and most American refineries are designed for Iraqi oil. So America got its oil and the Oil-for-Food Program was presented. Are the Iraqi people like worms to eat or sleep? If they cared about the Iraqi people, they would have lifted the embargo."

We then asked Saddam about Operation Desert Fox in

December 1998, the military operation ordered by the Clinton administration to punish Iraq after Saddam had expelled UN weapons inspectors. "I don't remember the details, but I remember the essence," he said. "It seemed there was a certain understanding of power in the U.S. leadership, that if they didn't attack Iraq, they had a weak president. So I used to joke about it, saying, 'This is our luck. Every new president has to take a whack at us!' So an old president was better for us than a new one. So I told the Revolutionary Command Council, 'Thank your lucky stars it was only four days of strikes that really didn't damage our industry.'" When asked about the effect of the bombing during Desert Fox, Saddam denied there was any. "One of the strange things—America would complain that its aircraft were attacked by Iraqi air defense. We used to talk among ourselves with pain and puzzlement. Not only did they violate Iraqi airspace—they were not flying over L.A., they were violating Iraqi sovereignty and violating UN Security Council [principles] that called for the respect of Iraqi sovereignty." Then Saddam used one of his patented counterfactual arguments. "There is not any WMD in Iraq or authorized by the leadership. You found a traitor who led you to Saddam Hussein. Isn't there one traitor who can tell you where the WMD is?" Saddam proceeded to lecture us about the great suffering caused by the embargo imposed by the UN Security Council after he invaded Kuwait in 1990 and left in place until he was forced from power in 2003.

Saddam was forever puzzled by his country's relationship with the United States. When we talked about U.S.–Iraqi relations, Saddam often got a perplexed look on his face, as if he was still trying to figure out where the relationship went wrong. "The West used to say good things about Saddam," he said. "But after 1990 all that changed." (Interestingly enough, this comment was echoed by officials from the George H. W. Bush administration during an NBC roundtable discussion on the twentieth anniversary of the Gulf War. Brent Scowcroft, who was national security adviser, said that after 1990, Saddam just changed. James Baker, the former secretary of state, shook his head in agreement. They couldn't understand why. Things had gone along well in the 1980s, but somehow Saddam changed. Saddam had remained remarkably consistent in his governing and his penchant for doing the unpredictable. The Bush 41 administration had been caught unaware by Saddam's foray into Kuwait. I strongly doubt that if Washington had made it clear to Saddam what it was willing to do to reverse any hostile Iraqi move against Kuwait, he would have crossed that red line.) Pointing out that America had supported Iraq during the Iran-Iraq War, Saddam said, "If I was wrong, why did the U.S. support me? If I was right, why did they change?" In Saddam's mind, it was the United States that had suddenly and inexplicably changed course. "Iraq had a good relationship with the U.S. in [President] Reagan's time, but it took a wrong turn during the [Bush] father and son era," he said. "I saw the day in the 1950s when Iraqi youth would line up for information about America. Now what does it look like? The embassies all have guns."

When discussing U.S.–Iraqi relations, Saddam would often circle back to what he saw as a Zionist conspiracy and Jewish control of U.S. institutions, particularly Congress and the news media. Saddam said the Western media had once given him good reviews, suggesting that the media were a weather vane of government attitudes. However, after 1990 and the invasion of Kuwait, all that changed. "Then the Zionists got involved and affected relations. The U.S. Congress stopped the export of grain to Iraq from the U.S. We explained it as Jewish influence and our stance on Palestine."

Although most analysts think the Iran-Iraq War ended in a stalemate, Saddam considered it a victory for Iraq, which he believed made it a target for the United States. According to Saddam, Iraq had a large army, an independent government, and a strong economy. And the United States could not tolerate a large Arab country dominating the region and threatening Israel. He thought that, with the demise of the Soviet Union, Washington was looking for enemies to fight to justify its large armies and weapons industries. Being the lone superpower created "a feeling of vanity in the American government. It was like a disease."

We returned to the subject of great leaders. For years at the CIA, I was told over and over again that he was a student of Stalin and Hitler, who were supposedly his role models. But Saddam had expressed admiration for de Gaulle, Lenin, Mao, and George Washington. Now he added Tito and Nehru. He was careful to note that he respected Lenin as a thinker. "Stalin does not interest me. He was not a thinker. For me, if a person is not a thinker, I lose interest. There were many stories about Stalin: his application on agricultural development and his dealings with owners and kulaks of large pieces of land, and Beria, his intelligence chief. It made him unfavorable, and his style was revolting."

Not once during our time together did Saddam say he admired Hitler or Stalin. The idea that Saddam was enthralled by Nazi and Soviet leaders gave many academics a template through which they could explain him to the layman. It was also an easy way to demonize the Iraqi strongman. This perception then migrated into the political world. On the eve of the Gulf War, President George H. W. Bush likened Saddam to Hitler. Once we have a new Hitler on our hands, it is incumbent on us to act. Why? Because the central lesson of Hitler's aggressive foreign policy was that the Allied nations chose appeasement when action might have stopped the German dictator and prevented World War II.

9.

Saddam Blows His Top

- - - - - - - - - -

After the first few debriefing sessions, Bruce came to me and asked me if I would take the lead in asking the questions. Whereas before we were both asking them, now I would be the sole questioner and Bruce's role would be simply to keep things going if Saddam looked like he was getting ready to cut off cooperation. With his limited knowledge of Saddam, he thought he had run out of provocative things to ask. By this time we had developed a regular routine for our debriefings. I said I would be happy to, even though I was feeling pretty exhausted after three months in Iraq. I'm a pretty sturdy guy, but poor eating, poor sleeping, and a grinding interview schedule of one or two sessions per day had taken a toll. I was feeling frustrated too. We had very little time to do research, and when we did, our computer bandwidth was so limited that it was impossible to delve into things that might have produced interesting answers. I suppose we could have simply gone through the motions of asking our questions and dutifully writing his answers down for the White House to read. But we were professionals, and this was the biggest thing going on in Iraq. I knew that it was unlikely I would ever get an opportunity like this again in my career. It was also unfamiliar territory for the Agency. Aside from the questioning of Panamanian strongman Manuel Noriega in 1989, U.S. government officials had not detained and questioned a former head of state since the end of World War II, when the U.S. interrogated Admiral Karl Doenitz, Hitler's chosen successor in the final days of the Third Reich.

Every morning we met with our military colleagues and were filled in on how Saddam was doing since we'd last seen him. I gave a brief rundown on what topics I planned to raise that day. Then we went to the debriefing cell and waited for him to be brought in. It had become clear that the FBI was not going to be taking over from us until after the New Year. When I asked the Bureau's representative in Baghdad why the FBI was taking so long, he just sort of shrugged his shoulders and said, "I guess they are just waiting for the holidays to be over." I figured the Bureau was still trying to put a team together and get up to speed on Saddam, who was not a run-of-the-mill FBI suspect. We were told the FBI was sending an Arabic-speaking special agent to be its team leader.

I looked at the list of topics we had already discussed and decided to bring the conversation back to something that Saddam had refused at first to discuss in detail. The chemical attack against Halabja, carried out in March 1988, was in retaliation for the Kurds' support of Iran and killed nearly five thousand people. The campaign was under the overall command of Saddam's paternal cousin, Ali Hasan al-Majid. Efraim Karsh and Inari Rautsi, authors of one of the better early biographies of Saddam, wrote: "Near the end of the Iran-Iraq war . . . more than half the villages and numerous towns in Kurdistan had been razed and their populations deported. Some half a million were placed in easily controllable settlements or in concentration camps in the south-western Iraqi desert." The specter of a major Iranian breakthrough in Kurdistan drove Hussein to employ gas on an unprecedented scale against the Kurdish town of Halabja. "As the thick cloud of gas spread by the Iraqi planes evaporated into the clear sky, television crews were rushed into the town by the Iranians and the world discovered the full extent of this horrendous massacre."[*]

Saddam didn't want to talk about Halabja, not only because it was classified as genocide but also because of his professed love for the Kurds. When I brought it up again, he got an angry look on his face and said, "Go ask Nizar al-Khazraji," the commanding officer on the ground at Halabja. When I told Saddam that Khazraji was not here but that Saddam was and that's why I was asking, he complained that this was interrogation and he would not submit to interrogation. I was disappointed because a discussion of Halabja could have told us a lot about Saddam, such as what he hoped to achieve and whether he fully understood the gravity of such a course of action, to name just two. I was determined to get him to talk about it. The gassing of the Kurds amounted to a crime against humanity—and was proof

---

[*]Efraim Karsh and Inari Rautsi, *Saddam Hussein: A Political Biography* (New York: Free Press, 1991), p. 169.

that Saddam had weapons of mass destruction and was willing to use them, even against fellow Iraqis.

In an effort to lower the temperature as I searched for another way to talk about Halabja, I changed the subject to the Revolutionary Command Council, the top governing political structure in Iraq. Saddam had been chairman of the RCC since 1979 and, while he was also president of the country, the RCC chairmanship was really the locus of power in the Ba'athist government. He responded that the RCC was the highest office constitutionally but then digressed into his usual observations that the National Assembly would make laws that sometimes would override the RCC. He said he wanted to encourage the proliferation of political parties in Iraq. This was a theme that Saddam harped on. He wanted to convince us that he was a true Iraqi democrat and that his efforts to bring plurality to Iraqi politics had been curtailed by the U.S. invasion. After another hour of conversation, I finally got Saddam to tell me that he was head of the Revolutionary Command Council and that his orders were necessary for RCC decisions to be approved.

This gave me the opening I had been looking for. I asked Saddam if the decision to use chemical weapons in Halabja originated in the RCC or somewhere else. Saddam was visibly furious. I had maneuvered him into a corner, and he was faced with either admitting that he had approved the attack or that he wasn't in complete control as he had just claimed. "What is your question?" he demanded. I replied, "Tell me about the decision to use chemical weapons at Halabja. Was this discussed at the RCC?" By this time, Saddam was so worked up that he was breathing heavily. Then he exploded: "When we heard about

Halabja, we thought the reports were Iranian propaganda. Therefore we did not discuss it in the RCC. We were always concerned about liberating our lands. You are saying that this was a decision made by Baghdad? If I choose to make this decision, then I will make that decision and I am not afraid of you or your president. I will do what I have to do to defend my country!"

He folded his arms to signal that the topic was closed, but then turned to me and sneered, "But I did not make that decision." At this point, we decided to close the briefing for the day, and as usual we tried to end it on an uncontentious note. I asked Saddam about some innocuous matter, but he was too angry to even try to reply. We called the guard, and as Saddam left the room, he glared at me, angrily put the hood over his head, and then jerked his arm up for the soldier to hold and guide him back to the cell. My boss was thrilled. We had finally gotten under Saddam's skin.

I have pissed off quite a few people in my life, but no one ever looked at me with such murderous loathing as Saddam did that day. He was under lock and key, but it was frightening even so. At the same time, something nagged at me about the exchange. I turned it over in my mind for months afterward. The more I thought about it, the more my gut told me that there was some truth in what Saddam had said. ████████████

████████████████████████████████

████████████████████████████████

████████████████████

Apparently Saddam had ceded control of chemical weapons to his commanders. Saddam first heard about the attack from his brother-in-law, Minister of Defense Adnan Khayrallah. Saddam was incensed. Not because his officers had used the weapons, but because they had used the weapons in territory held by Iranian sympathizers, and thus Iraq would not be able to control the news, while Iran would have a propaganda field day. I am not suggesting that Saddam was a softhearted, misunderstood leader. He made the decision to let his battlefield commanders use these weapons if they saw fit. He had already used chemical weapons to devastating effect against Iranian "human wave" attacks—something the U.S. government had turned a blind eye to because it was supporting Iraq. Saddam was not sorry about what had happened in Halabja. He showed no remorse. It was another example of what our government did not know—or chose not to know—as it built its case for his removal from power.

Abuse of human rights was a red line for Saddam. Once we brought it up, he would stiffen and prepare to do battle. I was usually the one who would raise the subject, and his eyes would narrow and he would try to deflect me any way he could. When I asked him about the discovery of mass graves, he leaned forward with a menacing look and said, "I explained that all before today when I explained about the governorates. I said that in circumstances like this it is not strange to find twenty here or forty there." (By this Saddam meant that he had lost control of fourteen of Iraq's eighteen governorates after the 1991 U.S. invasion and that he was not responsible for atrocities committed in territories that he did not control.) I then asked him about graves found in Basra, and he countered by demanding to know exactly where in Basra. When I told him they were found outside the city, he said, "Who are these people? What are their names?" I said I didn't have their names and Saddam threw his hands up in exasperation. If I didn't know their names, he said, then who was to say that these weren't the graves of Iranian soldiers? We went around and around on this for over an hour.

Saddam often tried to put a rosy gloss on what the world saw as acts of brutality. A case in point was his treatment of the Marsh Arabs, who were mostly Shiites. Saddam diverted the Tigris and Euphrates away from the marshes in retaliation for the Shia uprising after the Gulf War. The wetlands became desert, and nearly 150,000 Marsh Arabs were displaced. An estimated 80,000 to 120,000 fled to Iranian refugee camps, with the rest scattering elsewhere in Iraq. Saddam claimed he drained the marshes for their own good. "How can a person live on water?" he said with a mixture of incredulity and exasperation, despite being a man who supposedly loved water. "The land there is very fertile. I wanted to expand the agricultural land. Did you see how these people live? I lived with them for weeks, so I knew all the details. So I did the right thing for people and for strategic reasons . . . We built schools and clinics. We established electricity. Before that, it was like they were living three hundred years ago." He also said the marshes were drained to prevent Iranians from infiltrating into Iraq. Saddam drew a picture of the marshes and commented that Iraq was in the shape of a woman. The marsh areas crowded around Highway 1, connecting the southern areas of Iraq with Baghdad. The Iranians tried to cut off this road during the Iran-Iraq War.

One day I asked Saddam about his Ministry of Foreign Affairs, and we had a long and illuminating talk about how he operated bureaucratically. In 1998, he rotated diplomats and brought many ambassadors home to Baghdad. I asked him why he made the changes. He told me that there was no particular reason. He just thought it was time for some of the diplomats who had been out of the country for many years to return to Iraq. When I tried to tease out whether he had an ulterior motive, Saddam dismissed the idea. "I think you think that I have more power than I did." I asked in particular about the recall of Nizar Hamdun, who was his former representative to the United Nations and his most effective spokesman in the West. I said Hamdun understood the international system and the United States and knew how to use the media to get his message in front of the American public in a way few diplomats from the region could. Saddam agreed, but said Hamdun had cancer. "America is the best country for treating cancer, but we had issued a decree in the command that we won't send anyone from the Ministry of Foreign Affairs abroad for medical reasons. Personally, I was embarrassed, and the president can send people for treatment. So, since he was considered an old and loyal Ba'athist from before the revolution of July 1968, and was part of the group of people in which I had personal trust and knowledge, I sent him. So I . . . gave him five thousand dollars for the treatment. It was a personal gift to supplement his entitlement. He was not a friend. I did not have a large group of friends in the government. Having friendships with government personalities has problems and obligations. On the other hand, I considered all comrades and brothers if they were loyal and trustworthy. If you wanted to look into the human side of Saddam Hussein and how he treated his comrades, you could fill volumes." The five thousand dollars was a paltry sum, possibly because Saddam had no idea what cancer treatment cost in the United States, or more probably because he had soured on Hamdun after the diplomat had developed numerous close contacts in the U.S. government over the years.

Much has been made of the growing sectarian conflict in Iraq since the fall of Saddam. Indeed, Iraqi sectarianism has served as a template for the region. Under his regime, Saddam bragged repeatedly, there was no sectarianism. "Do you know if Saddam Hussein is Sunni or Shia? In front of the law they are both equal. In 1959, the secretary [of the Ba'ath Party] was a Shia from Nasiriyah. I found out years later and said I did not know that. In 1960–61 the secretary was a Kurdish Shia named Abd al-Karim al-Shaikhly. In 1965 the secretary was a Christian named Kildani. You talk of bodies found. They were not judged on being Sunni or Shia, but as those who would stand against the law."

Saddam was very proud of his leadership of the Ba'ath Party. "This is part of my nation. It calls for social justice, Arabic unity, freedom, and democracy. So as a young man, I found these goals were worth fighting for. All of my family members were in the party, except my uncle Khayrallah because he was very old." When asked if he'd ever felt lonely at the top, Saddam replied, "I am a commander but I visited the front and ate with the soldiers. I visited the front, so I never felt lonely." Saddam said he never envisioned ruling Iraq for long. "I thought that after the success of the 1968 revolution I could retire and leave the command on 30 July after the party took control. The RCC refused strongly and said, 'You had the revolution, so now you leave us stuck with it?' Again I wanted to retire in 1974 but my request was denied . . . Retirement meant abandoning principles, abandoning the people, and I stopped trying to retire after that."

I asked if the cult of personality surrounding him had hurt his ability to lead. Saddam replied, "I didn't tell them to put up my picture everywhere . . . Iraq was important before Saddam Hussein, and before Saddam Hussein's father, and before Saddam Hussein's grandfather. Iraq taught the world how to write, taught the world art, painting, and industry . . . So how could Saddam Hussein be more important than Iraq?"

When asked about his proudest accomplishments, Saddam said, "Building Iraq . . . from a country where people walked barefoot, illiteracy was 73 percent, small incomes, until the stage where we were so developed that the U.S. considered us a threat. Schools everywhere, hospitals everywhere, and personal income was very high before the war with Iran. Before 1991 electricity was in every village, and we built many roads . . . Even Americans who entered Iraq were impressed by the development. We served the people sincerely and we received Allah." After all this development, wasn't Saddam to blame for Iraq's decline? "Is it my responsibility to fight? Yes, it was my decision—Iran did not offer us peace. If Khomeini [had stopped at the border, instead of trying to grab portions of Iraqi territory], he would have won most of Iraqi public opinion . . . But he turned and showed his true colors and said his goal was to reach Karbala, not the border . . . But Kuwait was the nail in Iraq's foot. Iraq broke its horns in Kuwait." When asked where he saw Iraq in one hundred years, Saddam said, "It is in Allah's hands. I see Iraq liberated from the Americans in five years."

I spent my last session with Saddam talking about the history of Iraq. It was the shortest session I had with him, only twenty-five minutes. The real purpose was to tell him I was leaving and to introduce my replacement. We were concerned that Saddam might be upset by a new face and stop cooperating. We shouldn't have worried. Although Saddam had begun to tire of me, he hadn't tired of the process. That would come later. I spoke very warmly about our sessions and told Saddam how much I had enjoyed meeting him. Bruce told Saddam that Mr. Steve had to go back to the United States, and Mr. Bill would be my replacement. Saddam threw his hands in the air, vexed by having another interlocutor. "You mean I am going to have to answer the same questions all over again," he said. We told him that my replacement had read through all the reports and was well versed in what had been discussed so far. I then offered a short valedictory: "I want to thank you for engaging with us in our conversations about history. While there have been times we have disagreed on certain things, I appreciate your willingness to discuss them with us. I am sorry we had to meet under such circumstances. However, now that we have met, I feel that I understand you and your country better than I did. And for that, I thank you."

I stood and offered my hand to Saddam. What happened next really caught me by surprise. Saddam reached out, grabbed hold of my hand, and wouldn't let go. He then offered his parting statement to me: "I want you to know that I have enjoyed our time together as well. The reason you and I have disagreed is that you are where you are and I am here [Saddam motioned to his prison surroundings]. I am not some politician who goes around saying things for the sake of saying them. But I want you to listen to me when I say, as you go back to Washington and perform your very important work, I want you to remember to be just and fair. These are the noblest qualities that any human being possesses."

Saddam urged me to use my wisdom for good causes. I have a hard time remembering exactly what he said after that because I was in his grip and, for the first time since meeting him, I couldn't take notes. I was locked in his hard vise for the next five minutes or so. He was a politician and he was using his political skills on me as he said good-bye. People have asked me why he did this. Bruce and my replacement, Bill, both told me that Saddam barely acknowledged their departure and that was it. What made me special? Part of Saddam's send-off was an Arab custom to make guests feel that their stay was too short and their departure was causing pain. He clung to the idea that Iraq was his country and that we were only guests, and uninvited guests at that. Part of it, I think, was that Saddam had some measure of respect for me because I had spent years studying him before we ever met. He had learned that he needed to be on his guard with me and that I would challenge him if he took liberties with the facts. And part of it was probably relief. The pesky guy who kept bringing up massacres and human rights abuse was finally going away.

After I left Baghdad, Saddam became markedly more upbeat. He took an instant liking to Mr. Bill, my replacement. That was probably because Bill was also someone with a wealth of knowledge about Iraq that made the discussions lively and interesting for Saddam. Bill also had another attribute that Saddam liked: He didn't need to bring up human rights abuse or security-related issues because they had been thoroughly explored. That is not to say they didn't have their disagreements and moments of tension. They did. But their sessions were less confrontational.

Bill also had the advantage of not racing against the clock with headquarters breathing down his neck. When my team started debriefing Saddam, we were told for the first week or so that the FBI was going to arrive any moment and each session might be our last. As a result, we didn't have time to put Saddam at ease to possibly get him to speak more freely. We had to ask the tough questions right away. This forced us, especially me as the Iraq expert, to raise matters that upset him. After a while, this aggressiveness made me less effective. Because I had angered him with my questions about Halabja, Saddam became wary of me and constantly asked me why I wanted to know about a particular subject. The day after our Halabja conversation, when I tried to revisit some more questions about the Ministry of Foreign Affairs, he interrupted me and said, "Stop beating around the bush. Come to the point—what is it you want to know?" Our Halabja conversation had clearly struck a chord with Saddam and now his guard was way up and almost impossible to penetrate.

Soon after I left, the U.S. military asked Saddam to make a statement calling on Iraqi insurgents to lay down their arms. Admiral McRaven filled us in on the plan at my last morning meeting. We wished him luck but said we thought it unlikely that Saddam would agree. On January 13, 2004, McRaven approached Saddam as one senior commander speaking to another. McRaven's request carried no threat of execution, veiled or otherwise. But Saddam refused to sign or even read the statement. "My dignity does not allow me to read it," he said.

Later on, Saddam expanded on his refusal to Bill, my replacement: "I think that the military authorities didn't understand Iraq or Saddam Hussein or any of the people involved in this matter. This military commander . . . introduced himself as a historian and talked about Napoleon and Mussolini . . . But, you know, Napoleon's story is not our story; it's a different story. I understood that what he meant was just like Mussolini, I was to sign the letter or I would be executed. But, how old am I? So, how much longer am I going to live? You know, this method should not be used with Saddam Hussein. I should not be threatened; we should have a dialogue. When I speak of a dialogue, it's because I believe in dialogue, not because I am a prisoner. So the way to stop the bloodshed is dialogue—dialogue with me or with other members of the command who are captured. But the occupier who comes across the Tigris to our country and asks the occupied to stop fighting—that is not logical. We will say, 'If you want to stop the bloodshed, you should leave.' You will be losing nothing by leaving, but we will be losing everything if we stop fighting."[*]

---

[*]Debriefing notes, January 4, 2004.

10.

Deep Dive in the
Oval Office

When I got back to Washington, I was asked to go to the seventh floor at CIA headquarters to report on the debriefings. The most senior person scheduled to attend, Deputy Director of Intelligence Jami Miscik, could not make it, so I briefed her assistant. I was not summoned to meet with George Tenet or any of the other more senior officers.

After I briefed Miscik's assistant, I returned to my old post on the Iran desk. The chief of Iran Issue called me into his office and gave me the only reward I received for my interrogation of Saddam: a seventy-five-dollar gift certificate to a local Italian restaurant. It seemed that the Iran desk wanted to reward me but didn't want to give me too much, because everything I did was really for another office. For its part, the Office of Iraq Analysis didn't give me anything because I was not yet one of their own. The CIA, like most large bureaucracies, was plagued with competing fiefdoms. The only thing that really bothered me was that the Agency never formally expressed condolences on the death of my mother while I was in Iraq.

About two months after I got home, I got a call from the executive director's office. Buzzy Krongard, the third-ranking officer at the CIA and a confidant of George Tenet, asked to hear about my interrogation of Saddam. All that the brass wanted to know was where to find the WMD. Krongard was a curmudgeonly former Marine and, according to *The Washington Post*, liked to have people punch him in the gut to show how tough he was.[*]

He was a stickler for looking professional at work—a view, incidentally, that I shared—and I expected he would ask me what I wore during the debriefing. Krongard probably had a good idea of what I was going to say, because he had seen me in cargo pants and a Georgetown hoodie when he was in Baghdad. Even so, when I told him that I had dressed in fatigues and a sweatshirt, he blew up and said that he would have confronted Saddam in a three-piece suit. I tried to explain that the conditions were not conducive to wearing business attire. Often we were up to our ankles in mud when we walked to the prison. The military had asked us to keep a low profile, so as not to alert the outside world to Saddam's presence for fear of an escape or an assassination attempt. Krongard was scornful when I said I had a document that Saddam signed—a statement of how much money he had in his possession at the time of his arrest—and had surrendered it to FBI as evidence. "I bet you'd probably

---

*Vernon Loeb and Greg Schneider, "Colorful Outsider Is Named No. 3 at the CIA," *The Washington Post*, March 17, 2001, p. A3.

frame it and show it to your friends," he said with a hint of disgust in his voice. I explained that I would be lying if I said I didn't want to keep it, but that I also understood that we were to turn over anything that Saddam had signed to the FBI, which we did. After my briefing with Krongard, it was clear to me that the seventh floor had no clue what we had been up against—or what it took to conduct a successful debriefing.

In Iraq, I had the most remarkable experience an analyst could have. I say this with great humility because there were many young men and women who did more important things under far more trying circumstances. Readjusting to the deskbound routines of Langley was a jolt. Still, it felt good to be back in the United States, and I wanted to get my career back on a good track. I stayed on the Iran desk until July 2004, when I began a year as the director of leadership analysis at the Sherman Kent School, the Directorate of Intelligence training academy for newly hired officers. Then I returned to the Iran desk until late 2005.

Earlier in 2005, the seventh floor had put out another urgent request for analysts willing to go to Iraq. The first few deployments of analysts—measured mostly in three- and six-month increments—had come and gone, and the war showed no signs of abating anytime soon. The memo stated explicitly that if you were an analyst and wanted to do your patriotic duty to help your country in wartime, then now was the time to volunteer. In reality, most managers, other than those in the Office of Iraq Analysis, didn't support the war and didn't want their analysts to help fight it. When I approached my Iran team chief about returning to Iraq, she said I would lose all chance of being promoted if I went. In classic bureaucratic fashion, the manager of Iran Issue supported her. This made me all the more determined to go. So in 2006 I volunteered to return to the Iraq beat.

As senior analyst on the Iraq leadership team, I was teamed up with more than a dozen analysts, most of them barely out of college. For the most part, they weren't planning a career at the CIA and considered the Agency a stepping-stone to more lucrative jobs. When I first started at the CIA, analysts were brought in one or two at a time. That way they could get intensive training and supervision. After the invasion, the CIA brought in new Iraq analysts by the truckload. To say they were green would be putting it mildly. Few of them had analytic skills, and most were content to cut and paste material from previously published intelligence reports, or the raw data from electronic intercepts, or reports from the National Clandestine Service.

I devoted myself to a subject considered one of the most important to the White House in 2006: Muqtada al-Sadr. Despite his pudgy, unprepossessing appearance, Sadr had a large and loyal following among Shiites in Iraq by virtue of the fact that he was the son and son-in-law of two ayatollahs who had been assassinated by Saddam's hit squads. Sadr had been a thorn in the side of the Bush administration since the overthrow of Saddam. I first started studying Sadr when General George W. Casey Jr., commander of the coalition forces until 2007 (he would spend the next four years as the Army's chief of staff), asked for a paper comparing him to Hasan Nasrallah, the charismatic and cunning leader of Hezbollah, the Lebanon-based Shia militants known as the best-trained and best-equipped guerrilla fighters in the region.

I was immediately struck by the condescending and derisive way the U.S. intelligence community viewed Sadr. It was sometimes said that he aspired to be Iraq's Nasrallah but fell far short of his communication and leadership skills. That was true, but the United States seriously underestimated Sadr by dismissing him as a crazy, thuggish killer who passed the time playing video games. My office was still using an outdated profile of him written in 2003 by a very junior analyst.

In the meantime, Sadr had repeatedly called for coalition forces to leave Iraq. After coalition authorities closed his newspaper, *Al-Hawza*, on incitement charges in March 2004, Sadr's Mahdi Army turned to violence, killing dozens of foreign soldiers and Sunnis. When Paul Bremer, chief of the Coalition Provisional Authority, called Sadr an outlaw on April 5, 2004, the Shia cleric declared a jihad against the coalition. Four days later, his army ambushed military convoys trying to get in and out of the Baghdad airport. We had a lot of current intelligence on Sadr, but most of it was flimsy. By 2006, when Sadr's army was a fighting force feared both by Sunnis and U.S. soldiers, we should have had a robust body of work ready to give to policymakers.

When I began to dig into the reporting, I was shocked to find no mention of Muqtada's father, Muhammad Sadiq al-Sadr. He was killed in 1999 during my first stint as a leadership analyst on Iraq, and the riots following his death were the greatest threat to Saddam's rule since the Shia uprisings in southern Iraq after the Gulf War. Nobody seemed to grasp the profound effect his murder had on Muqtada and Iraqi Shiites. There was no in-depth background look on what Sadr hoped to achieve or his standing in the religious community. Worse still, there was no study of Sadr's relationship with the Najaf *hawza*, the Shia seminary led by Ali Sistani, the most influential religious and political leader in post-invasion Iraq.

I began writing a number of reports that looked at Sadr and what he was trying to do. I knew that the link between father and son was key and that millions of Shiites who had revered Muhammad Sadiq al-Sadr had transferred their support to his son. I had a lot of trouble getting people to understand that a Shia leader who suffers on their behalf often means as much to them after his death as he did when he was alive. Toward the end of 2007, I was called into my group chief's office and told that the White House wanted a "deep dive" on the cleric—a fifteen-to-twenty-minute briefing for the president in the Oval Office. A paper on a deep-dive topic was often produced and given to the White House over the weekend so that the president and vice president would have time to read it and receive a briefing on it first thing Monday morning. My heart skipped about three beats. I was going to do something I had always wanted to do: go to the Oval Office and brief the president. Finally, I thought, I could bring my knowledge to bear in a way that would be important.

While it is somewhat misleading to call this exercise a deep dive, it was still a badge of honor for an analyst. I worked doggedly on my paper. I concluded that Muqtada al-Sadr was having a difficult time adjusting to life in Iran, where he had taken temporary refuge in January 2007 just ahead of the surge in U.S. forces to Iraq, but he would remain a potent force in Iraqi politics if he did not stay in Iran too long. The reporting led me to believe that he was unsure of what to do next and how to remain relevant to what was going on inside Iraq.

My group chief and I were in full accord on this, and most of the people who saw the report gave it high marks. The paper went through layers of editing—by the team chief, then by the group chief, then by the front office of the Office of Iraq Analysis. From there it went up to the editors of the president's daily briefing. Then I was put through a "murder board," at which experts try to anticipate any questions that might arise at the White House. My manager, Larry, decided I needed more practice before I went downtown. I went through two more murder boards. New information flowed in every day, so I had to constantly update my paper.

The preparation for the deep dive—whiteboarding ideas for the paper, writing the paper, murder boards—went on for weeks before my Oval Office meeting. It was on February 4, 2008, the Monday after the Super Bowl. I got up at two a.m. to be at Langley by four a.m. Once there, I logged on to my computer to see if anything had happened overnight in Iraq that would need to be included in my report. I went up to the seventh floor to give a final review of my paper and answer any questions that the briefers may have had before they set out in the early morning hours to brief their principals. (The CIA provides daily intelligence briefings to members of the president's national security team as well as to the president and vice president.) Then I went downtown with the analyst who briefs the director of national intelligence (DNI), in this case Admiral Mike McConnell. We went to his office in the Old Executive Office Building, and I gave him a summary of what I planned to say.

He seemed pleased with my take. He then showed me where to sit in the Oval Office. By the time I got to the White House, I had been up for five hours and was starting to get hungry and thirsty. From 7:50 to 8:30, I sat with another analyst in an alcove outside the Oval Office and silently rehearsed my pitch.

It's a surreal atmosphere when you're queued up to talk to the most powerful man in the world. The waiting room is filled with a lot of busy-looking people who tend to walk by very fast. We saw some of the luminaries of the administration as they ducked into the president's office. Then came a White House steward carrying a tray of Diet Cokes. The tray was marked with the presidential seal, as were the bottles. Life inside the bubble.

Finally, an aide came out and said to us, "The president is ready for you now." When I walked in, I saw I would be seated on a couch to the right of the vice president. Both President Bush and Vice President Cheney were sitting in wingback chairs perpendicular to the position of the couch. Also in the room were my fellow analyst Karen, Admiral McConnell, National Security Adviser Stephen Hadley, and the CIA briefer. I sat down and the president said, "Shoot. Give me what you got."

I began my prepared remarks, but I got only halfway through before the president began interrupting me with questions. I had seen him shortly after the 2000 election recount, and I was stunned by how he had aged in the seven years since. We talked about Sadr for a few minutes. The president was fully engaged and interested in the paper we had prepared. Bush said the paper was exactly the kind of thing he hoped to see, because it told him a great deal about Muqtada that he hadn't known. He even made a joke about how both he and Muqtada struggled under famous fathers. That Sadr was having problems keeping his movement under control and was unhappy living in Iran was probably the first bit of good news about him that the White House had gotten since 2004. The president clearly disdained Sadr, who had become our new Iraqi bogeyman. During our conversation he asked me if we should have killed Sadr. I said that would only make him a martyr and add to his popularity.

At this point the DNI mentioned that I was the first to debrief Saddam Hussein. Bush looked at me and said, "How many of you guys were the first to debrief him?" That was my first taste of the president's brand of humor. I said I didn't know if Saddam had met with anyone before me, but that I was the first CIA person to talk with him. Bush then asked me what my job was in Baghdad. I told him that I had served as the High Value Target No. 1 analyst. "Were you at the embassy?" the president asked. I told him there was no embassy at the time, only the CPA headquarters. He asked me if I knew George Piro, the special agent who had done the FBI's debrief of Saddam and who had been the subject of a *60 Minutes* profile a few weeks earlier, and I told him we had never met.

He then asked me what kind of man Saddam was. I told him that he was very disarming at first and used humor and a self-deprecating wit to try to put you at ease. Bush got a look on his face that suggested he was going to lose it. I quickly explained that these were only tactics and that the real Saddam, the one I got to know, was sarcastic and arrogant, aside from being a cruel and sadistic man. That seemed to calm Bush down. He looked over at Cheney during this time and their eyes locked in a knowing way. Bush wanted to know why Saddam didn't take our offer to leave Iraq; on March 17, 2003, Bush addressed the American people to announce that he had given Saddam forty-eight hours to leave the country before the United States would attack and bring down his regime. I explained that Saddam felt safe only in Iraq and also didn't believe that the United States would be able to withstand a punishing war. Bush asked me if Saddam knew he was going to be executed. I told him that one of the first things Saddam said was that he knew his imprisonment would lead to his execution and that he was at peace with that. Bush then said Saddam would have a lot to answer for in the next life.

Overall, what usually was a ten-to-fifteen-minute session lasted about thirty minutes. It was both exhilarating and exhausting. It was exhilarating because I was talking to the president of the United States. It was exhausting because of the intensity of the experience, the need to be on full alert every second, the weeks of preparation, and the lack of sleep and nourishment over the previous five hours. By the end of the session, I was just running on adrenaline. Finally the president thanked us and we were dismissed. As I was leaving, he smiled and said to me, "You sure Saddam didn't say anything about where he put those vials of anthrax?" and everyone laughed. I responded that he didn't and, if he had, the president would have been the first to know. It was a lame response, but I thought his crack was inappropriate considering that the United States had already lost more than four thousand men and women, with tens of thousands injured.

When I got back to headquarters, I went to the morning briefing on the seventh floor and gave a summary of the Oval Office meeting. Everyone was all smiles because the president was pleased with my paper. I was relieved that the session was over and happy that the briefing was well received. But I was a little disconcerted by how much the Agency brass wanted to please the president.

I was then asked to write a paper on Saddam's interrogation that my office presented in the Oval Office in March 2008. In April, I was invited to discuss Saddam's debriefing with Cheney, who had had an earlier White House session on the subject. I prepared my usual presentation of what it was like to debrief Saddam and what the takeaways were, and went to the vice president's office with Bill, the CIA analyst who had succeeded me in Baghdad, and George Piro. A number of Cheney's aides were also present, including David Addington and John Hannah. I had heard a great deal about these two and had briefed Hannah once before. I knew him to be well informed but not without an ideological side. Addington I had never met. I knew him only by reputation, which was controversial to say the least.

Many critical things have been said about Cheney. He was called Darth Vader, and critics viewed him as the source of evil in the Bush administration. In my few dealings with him, I found him to be professional, dignified, and considerate. He looked to me to lead the briefing. I said that he had already heard about some of my experiences, I knew his time was short, and, in the interest of hearing from all of us, Bill would kick things off. Bill gave an overview of the CIA debriefings in a concise and judicious way. After that, the three of us shared our observations with the group. Piro embarked on a rather long soliloquy psychologizing Saddam, saying he saw him as a "conditional thinker," whatever that meant. I think Cheney was equally nonplussed. He asked probing questions without ever letting on what he was looking for. He was a consummate political player, who was an expert at hiding his cards.

Cheney had a human side that few people got to see. and he smoothed the way for free and easy discussions. I never got the feeling that he was pushing for a particular answer; he wanted to hear what you had to say. It was after you left the room that Cheney would tell the president what he thought, and his conclusions would perhaps be at odds with what you'd said. But he was an attentive listener, something Bush was not. At one point Cheney asked about one of Saddam's aides, and we told him that Saddam didn't like having people around him who were smarter than he was, and consequently employed a lot of people with lesser skills. Cheney laughed and said he operated the same way, bringing guffaws from the aides in the room.

Another telling exchange came when the vice president opened things up for questions from his staff. It was clear that our briefing was for the record and that his memoir was very much on Cheney's mind. The aides bombarded us with questions: What were the links between Saddam and the first World Trade Center bombing? What were Saddam's relations with the Palestinian terrorist Abu Nidal? What did Saddam say about his support for martyrdom operations in Israel? What did he say about supporting the PLO? Did Saddam talk about his connections to al-Qaeda? What did he say about the meetings between Osama bin Laden and Farouk Hijazi, a high-ranking official in the Iraqi Intelligence Service who met with bin Laden in the mid-1990s and later became Iraq's ambassador to Turkey? What about WMD? Did Saddam plan to reconstitute his weapons?

On and on they went, asking all the hot-button terrorism questions that we had answered over and over in the past. The briefing was supposed to be only a half hour but lasted more than ninety minutes.

11.

Crosswise with the President

A few months later I was asked to go back to the White House for another deep dive. However, my role in this meeting was to back up the Gulf analyst who would be talking to the president about trends among the region's Shiites. I would be there to handle any questions related to Iraq or Iran. We did everything we always did before such meetings. A paper was written and fully vetted. We held our murder board meeting and gave our presentation to the seventh floor so the brass would know what we were going to say. But no matter how hard you prepare, you never know how things are going to go. As it turned out, this was one of the most painful—and one of the most fascinating—experiences I had while working for the Agency.

The meeting was scheduled for May 8, 2008, and I was looking forward to it. I thought to myself, "I'll go to the Oval Office and sit with the high and mighty again and finally get a chance to take a look around and absorb the surroundings." I was so keyed up on my prior visit that I couldn't even remember what the Oval Office looked like. I didn't feel the same pressure "backbenching" the primary analyst (even though I had almost no background on some of the more controversial points in my colleague's paper). There was a big section on "Iranian support for terror," and I was told to be prepared to answer questions about that. Why someone from Iran Issue was not going I'll never know, except that most of their analysts were new and untested. So I dug into the subject in hopes that I could give authoritative answers.

As the day approached, I began to feel even more confident about the Oval Office briefing. I was now steeped in the Iran terror issue and felt sure I could give an intelligent answer to almost any question. I woke up at three a.m. to get ready for the ride to the CIA and then to the White House. I got my first inkling that it was going to be a screwy morning when I went to the seventh floor to see the briefers and they asked me about a report that had come in overnight that seemed pretty important. I could tell at a glance that the report seemed odd and at variance with everything I knew about the subject. Therefore, I gave it very little credibility. I then rode downtown with the briefer for the director of National Intelligence.

DNI Mike McConnell had seemed gruff in our first meeting, but he was actually a nice man faced with an impossible job—reining in an out-of-control intelligence community and dealing with a president who reputedly bullied his staff and advisers. Sad to say, someone of McConnell's temperament was not suited to the bare-knuckle work of the DNI. He seemed pleased when we went over our presentation. But he appeared miffed when I told him I was going only as a "backbencher." He said that I had to be prepared to say something, so I gave him my analytic line on the paper that we were presenting. I think he may have thought that I was unprepared, which couldn't have been further from the truth. Looking back on it, I again thought it was crazy to be sending an analyst to be the secondary briefer on a topic that was not his usual area of competency. In any event, McConnell said the president was very busy and probably would not have much time for us. He said we would be in the Oval Office for no more than five minutes and told me to expect a question about Muqtada al-Sadr.

After a short wait, we were ushered into the Oval Office. The president and vice president seemed to recognize me and said hello. All the people attending the briefing had a glass of water or a Diet Coke in front of them except the two who needed them the most—the briefers. My colleague Greg launched into a summary of his paper on the Gulf Shiites and immediately got peppered with questions from the president. The president looked annoyed, distracted, and uninterested. This was the week his daughter Jenna was getting married. He also was getting ready for a big trip to the Middle East, from which he would return just before the wedding. I don't think he had read the briefing paper the night before, as he usually did. He seemed put out when I brought up the subject of Sadr and the possibility he would move to Saudi Arabia. Bush said that King Abdullah didn't like Sadr and that the only reason he let him into Saudi Arabia was to perform the hajj, the annual Islamic pilgrimage to Mecca. (This was probably more a case of an Arab leader telling the president what he wanted to hear. King Abdullah was not above trying to flatter Sadr and at times gave him much-needed financial help.)

Bush then told me that Adil Abdul-Mahdi, a member of the Islamic Supreme Council of Iraq, had told him that Sadr was practically "retarded." I said that I had heard comments about Sadr like that before, but that Abdul-Mahdi was an enemy of Sadr and that their bad blood might color his view. The president had not factored in that Iraqi rivals might badmouth each other to gain advantage with the United States. Bush seemed to think that Iraqis would not lie to him after he had saved their country from the clutches of a tyrant. I was surprised by his naiveté, because the president was an intelligent man, not the lazy C student caricatured in the media. I could tell by talking to him that he read a lot of the cable traffic and raw intelligence reports. During our briefing he recalled the name of a participant in a meeting with Grand Ayatollah Ali Sistani when that name escaped me. He appeared to be able to retain information and had good recall of intelligence reporting; he just had trouble coming up with what to make of it.

After five minutes of this, Bush got a bored look on his face, put the paper down, and said, "OK, so what you're telling me is that everything is OK, right?" Greg, the Gulf analyst, said that was correct. Bush then replied, "OK, what's up with Sadr?" and looked at me. Sadr was a source of constant interest in the Bush White House. Even though I had briefed the president on Sadr in February, he wanted an update on the cleric. To be honest, I had prepared to answer questions that pertained to the paper that had been given to the president. The president's request for a briefing caught me by surprise. I was fully up on the latest developments relating to the Iraqi cleric, but now I was being asked to put together a polished presentation in less than thirty seconds and be prepared to answer whatever questions were fired at me. Now, this was not as easy as it may sound. Whenever the CIA went to the Oval Office to do a deep dive on a particular subject, we produced a paper that would help frame the discussion. This was very important because Bush had a tendency to start firing questions at the briefer that went in multiple directions. Having the paper as the point of departure helped keep the president within the framework of the discussion at hand.

The president had completely changed the focus of our meeting. We would no longer discuss Greg's topic. Now the president wanted a briefing on an entirely new subject: Sadr. Suddenly I found myself briefing the president without the paper and without the necessary framework that would be needed to keep him focused. In March 2008, Prime Minister Nuri al-Maliki had attacked the Sadrists in Basra and, despite almost being surrounded by the Sadrist militias, was able to deal a stern blow against the cleric's gunmen. I wasn't ready for a detailed discussion of Sadr, because I had spent most of my prep time working on Iranian terrorism to support Greg's presentation. Suddenly, all eyes were on me and I had to wing it. I swallowed hard and said, "Well, that is the sixty-four-thousand-dollar question, isn't it?" I was not trying to be funny. I merely said it to give myself five more seconds so I could come up with an answer. Bush looked at me and said, "Well, why don't you make it the seventy-four-thousand-dollar question, or whatever your salary is, and answer the question!" I thought to myself, "What an asshole!"

Here I was in the Oval Office, the place where McGeorge Bundy used to brief JFK and LBJ. I had always thought this was the place where you discussed weighty issues in a serious and deliberative way. I said "Understood, sir," and proceeded to piece together my briefing as I went along. Keep in mind that I was the only analyst in the room who could speak to this issue; usually, the Agency sent two analysts to cover a topic. I told the president about possible Iranian efforts to prosecute Sadr over the 2003 murder of a rival cleric. Bush seemed to get a kick out of this and guffawed: "Who'd have thought the Iranians would put the screws to Sadr." He asked me why they were doing this, and I told him that the Iranians had been looking for a way to get leverage over Sadr and keep him in line with their own intentions. This led the president to ask where all this was going. I said that Sadr might surprise us all, that he still had a substantial following and might be more resilient than we had thought. Bush looked at me in a funny way and asked if I thought that Sadr could play a constructive role in Iraq or be reconciled to the Maliki government. I said it was possible but unlikely in the current political environment.

Bush then told me that Sadr was a punk and a thug and someone the United States didn't have to deal with anymore. I responded that Sadr represented the views of a large number of Iraqis and could move big crowds when he wanted to. The president asked what evidence I had for this. I said Sadr recently told his followers not to demonstrate for fear they would spark violence. Bush countered that he had seen reports saying Sadr said this because he knew no one would show up for the demonstrations. This was news to me—I couldn't imagine where he had come across such claptrap—but I didn't pursue the point. Frankly, I was stunned that the president wanted to argue with me. I kept looking over at the CIA briefer to get her to shut down the session. She, or more likely the DNI, should have explained that the CIA was here to brief on the Shiites and could arrange a deep dive on Sadr later. However, both she and the DNI sat there like a bumps on a log. Everyone seemed afraid to say the wrong thing to Bush, including his senior advisers.

Bush's national security team could see that the president was confused, from the way he reacted to what I was saying. They then proceeded to circle the wagons around the president, attacking me as a hostile outsider. Defense Secretary Robert Gates simply swatted away what I was saying. "Oh, Mr. President, we feel that Sadr is not a threat anymore. He says one thing one day, another on another day. He's all over the place, and what he says doesn't matter." I interjected that Sadr had been very consistent with his messaging about opposing the United States and was, in fact, becoming more sophisticated in his ability to rally his followers. Condoleezza Rice said to me, "But don't you think he is just a flake? Why should anyone take him seriously anymore?" I said, "With all due respect, Madam Secretary, I have been hearing this for five years now, and by attaching labels like 'flake' to Sadr, I think we do ourselves a disservice by underestimating him." Bush broke in and practically screamed at me, "Oh, yeah? Well, I think we overestimate him! The man's a thug and a killer, and the Iraqi people don't want that."

At the end of the day, the president said, the future belonged to freedom. The Iraqi people wanted security for their families and the right to earn a decent living for themselves. And they were tired of Sadr killing them. Bush then asked me what I thought of that. I agreed that it was true that Sadr's Mahdi Army had certainly hurt itself with its violent behavior, but that religion mattered a great deal to the followers of Sadr. I added that Muqtada, along with his revered father, Muhammad Sadiq, enjoyed an almost iconlike status among Iraqi Shiites, who were, after all, the majority of the Iraqi population. I remember thinking how ironic it was that I had to explain to the president, a religious man, how important religion was in Iraq.

At this point, Admiral Michael Mullen, the chairman of the Joint Chiefs of Staff, jumped into the fray. He had read that some of Sadr's associates had told the cleric that they had dreams of pictures of his father with bleeding eyes. Mullen looked at me and asked, "What the hell are they all talking about?" I explained that it was not uncommon for Sadr to express himself that way or for his advisers to do the same. I said that Sadr was prone to mysticism, that he was studying to be an ayatollah, and that he often saw things through the prism of his father's experiences. I explained that dreams in Islamic culture are viewed differently than they are in the West. We regard dreams almost as hallucinations, while among Shiites dreams are sometimes seen as having a real effect on events or as portents to be taken seriously. I said that I had talked with some people who had known Sadr's father, and they spoke of him with a reverence and awe that was similar to the way in which some Sunnis used to talk about Saddam Hussein.

Bush looked at me with disbelief. "Reverence and awe?" he thundered, as if he couldn't believe his ears. Then he chuckled and looked at his advisers and said, "What Iraqis were you talking to?" and everyone laughed with the president. I explained that there were Iraqis to that day who still gathered at the grave of Saddam Hussein to remember him. I decided to tell the president about some of the Iraqis I had talked to. One in particular, whom I had debriefed in 1998, was a former aide to Uday Hussein. I explained that the man was articulate, spoke English well, understood international politics, and knew how to maneuver in Saddam's political system. He also believed that Saddam and Uday could read minds. I tried to use this as an example of what Iraqis were like, particularly Iraqis who had been traumatized by the arbitrary use of terror inflicted on them.

The president just laughed and said, "Maybe we can get a few mind readers in here." Bush's prep-school humor was a little hard to take. With his black-and-white view of the world, he couldn't accept the possibility that any Iraqi revered the deposed dictator.

Bush kept asking me whether I thought Sadr could be a constructive player in Iraq or whether he would always be at odds with the United States. I said that his father was anti-American and that Muqtada tended to hold the same beliefs. "Why didn't his father like us?" the president asked. I mentioned that the elder Sadr had condemned the Gulf War and American policy toward Israel. At that, Bush just rolled his eyes and motioned for me to stop. I said Sadr could probably be both a constructive player and a nuisance. I knew that was not the answer Bush wanted to hear. I had been told beforehand that the president wanted clear-cut opinions and didn't care if you were wrong; he just didn't want equivocations. I explained that Sadr in the short term would probably continue to harbor anti-U.S. views. But once back in Iraq, he would probably harbor anti-Tehran sentiments that could work in America's favor.

Bush leaned over and asked me again, "Should we have killed him?" He had asked me this question in our first meeting in the Oval Office and had asked it of several other analysts. I don't know why he kept harping on it, or why he would ask a GS-14 if the United States should break the law. I replied, "No, we should not kill him. Killing him would only make him a martyr and rally more people to his movement." I cautioned the president that in dealing with issues and people in the Middle East, it's hard to put them into neatly defined boxes, such as whether someone was a clear friend or foe. People in the region often didn't fit into any category and sometimes did contradictory things at the same time.

"Well, what's the answer?" he asked. "What should I do?" I said that while it was hard to take a passive approach, Sadr could be his own worst enemy. Without the United States as bogeyman, he might make a mistake that could cost him his leadership. Bush looked at me and said, "There were people who said that I should let Saddam be Saddam, and I proved them wrong." I wanted to say, "And that worked out so well?" But I just said, "Yes, you did, sir."

We had been talking about Sadr, but it could have been Saddam. After more than seven years in office, Bush had assiduously studied his Iraq brief but still didn't understand the region and the fallout from the invasion. A colleague who had briefed him told me that Bush was reading David Fromkin's 1989 book *The Peace to End All Peace: The Making of the Modern Middle*

East. It's a fascinating study of how the Allied powers became embroiled in the Middle East during World War I and carved up the region into spheres of influence with little or no regard to the ethnic or sectarian tensions that might result. One would think that a president with this level of intellectual curiosity would have thought long and hard before loosing the dogs of war. But Bush was reading the book in 2007—not in 2002, before he placed the United States into the ruinous conflict in Iraq.

Finally, a voice of reason in the room piped up. It was none other than Dick Cheney, who wanted to know about Grand Ayatollah Ali Sistani. We talked a bit about his health—in 2004, Sistani went to London for treatment of a heart condition—and how he had urged Shiites to practice moderation in the face of Sunni violence. Both the president and the vice president seemed interested. The hostile mood lessened once we got off the topic of Sadr. They asked me who I thought might succeed Sistani. I told him that we thought Grand Ayatollah Muhammad Ishaq al-Fayyad al-Afghani was the most likely candidate. Bush laughed again and said, "Ha, an Afghani. That'll teach 'em!" Once again, everyone laughed, at which point the president announced to me and my fellow briefer, "That is all, gentlemen," and we were dismissed.

As I walked out of the Oval Office, Josh Bolten, Bush's chief of staff, stood holding the door for us. He locked eyes with me and smiled, giving me a look like "Wow, you got the treatment." I got out of the room and said to Greg, "What the hell just happened in there?" I had never experienced a grilling like that from the president of the United States. Greg said to me, "You were great. There is no way I could have handled any of those questions. You fielded them well." I wasn't so sure. McConnell looked pretty annoyed with me as we left. I knew that the president wasn't pleased, and I feared that this was going to be a problem once I got back to CIA headquarters.

We traveled back in the car with the CIA briefer, and I asked her how she thought it had gone. She hemmed and hawed and said, "It was all right, I guess." Not much of a vote of confidence. The last time I had briefed the president, the briefer had been effusive in his praise. After I got back to Langley, I told my office about the session, and my colleagues couldn't hide their concern. To careerists, it didn't matter what you said as long as you made the president happy. I then went to the seventh floor to fill in the brass. I told them it was a spirited discussion and left it at that. I saw their nervous looks, and no one wanted me to stay for a longer discussion.

I then got word that CIA director Mike Hayden had been told that things hadn't gone well and that the president was upset. The day was such a whirlwind—after going to the Oval Office, I then had to go to the Pentagon to brief Undersecretary of Defense Eric Edelman—that I didn't get a chance to write up my own report of how the meeting went. The next day I had to write a memo for the president's daily briefing and again didn't have time to pull together my notes about our meeting. Then I noticed something strange: No one was asking for them. I realized that the only way to protect myself was to write them up and get my version of things into management's hands. I quickly banged out a memo for the seventh floor.

The one bit of good news came when Mike Morell, the CIA deputy director, sent a note to my management saying he thought

I had been put in an extremely difficult situation but had handled myself well. At the time, none of my managers shared this note with me; they preferred to keep me in the dark and let me dangle above their disapproval. When I walked around headquarters during the next few weeks, it was if I were radioactive. Only close colleagues talked to me. I felt like a modern-day Trotskyite, someone in an old Soviet photograph who had been airbrushed out of the picture because of a doctrinal dispute. When I later heard about Morell's message, I was grateful for the support from someone who understood the pressures analysts face.

I had an opportunity to go back to the Oval Office in the waning days of the administration. I chose not to, and I later felt terrible that I hadn't gone. Here I was, with an opportunity to once more meet with the president, and I let someone else take my spot. Going a third time would have been a feather in my cap. But I was not sure how much of an impact my paper would make on a president with roughly forty-five days left in his term. And most important, I didn't want to get the same treatment I received the last time. I felt that if the president saw me, it would be like waving a red cape at a bull. It is sad enough to think how much of taxpayer money gets wasted by the intelligence community, but it's even sadder when the president dismisses all this expensive work when it doesn't support his political views.

12.

In the Shadow of His Father

M y trips to the Oval Office were part of a new policy insti-
tuted in late 2007. The president continued to get his usual
intelligence briefing every morning, but the White House also
requested that the CIA send analysts to brief the president on a
host of Iraq-related issues. The reasoning behind this change
may have been the president's own frustration with what he was
getting from his briefer, or it may have been that Bush and his
advisers simply wanted unfiltered views. This was late in the day
for a change in the process, and how much it would affect the
U.S. policy in Iraq was anyone's guess. But it was a sign that the
administration knew its policies were not succeeding.

The administration's invitation to give the CIA greater access to the Oval Office represented a radical change. The Bush
team had been hostile to the experts during the run-up to the
war. The CIA had fared even worse during the previous administration. President Clinton distrusted the Agency and kept it at

arm's length, and analysts were rarely invited to the White House to brief the president. The morning briefings were handled by Sandy Berger, the president's national security adviser.

Bush's invitation was music to the Agency's ears. The CIA lives at the beck and call of the president and is always thinking of ways to serve his needs. This meant we would be getting much more time with him and more opportunities to prove our worth to our number one customer. Under the new regime, the Office of Iraq Analysis would send a senior person to the White House every Monday to brief the president on Iraq.

But greater access didn't necessarily mean the president would be better informed. In typical CIA fashion, the Agency let the White House choose the topic to be discussed. This was the "service" approach that managers at the CIA had adopted as their "best practice" even before Bush took office. As the conflict with Iraq loomed, the service approach became even more entrenched. It can work wonders if the policymaker is steeped in the issues, knows which questions to ask, and is brave enough to make decisions regardless of their political impact. But the service approach can have disastrous results when a president has strong preconceptions, a short attention span, and little time until the next election. I always felt that deciding what was important should be the job of the analysts, because policymakers are often too busy to know what they should be focusing on. But the pooh-bahs at the CIA felt that letting the White House choose the topic would let the Agency escape criticism if something went wrong. The CIA could say it supplied the requested information and blame the policymaker if the United States was tripped up by unforeseen events. But the more I read about past foreign policy fiascoes, the more I saw that the CIA was always the first to be blamed. So in a sense, we were damned if we did and damned if we didn't.

Under the service approach, the CIA disseminated up-to-the-minute intelligence to the policy world. This is the crack cocaine for consumers of classified information. It was presented in pithy one-page memos that went downtown every morning and described the latest developments in hot spots of interest. The analyses were by nature tactical and not terribly deep, but they scratched the itch of the policymakers who wanted to know the latest blips on any given subject. It enabled the busy policymaker to appear smart and current without doing a lot of reading or even giving an issue much thought. This approach sacrificed the strategic context that's so critical when it comes to making clear-sighted foreign policy. In effect, we provided intel fixes without telling policymakers where an issue was headed or what outcomes to expect. My friends at the CIA tell me that this remains one of the most glaring shortcomings of the intelligence apparatus.

I was an enthusiastic supporter of Bush in 2000. I had been deeply troubled by the Clinton administration's handling of foreign affairs—I thought President Clinton's attention to foreign policy was similar to that of a child with attention deficit disorder. Clinton seemed interested in foreign policy only when it could help bolster his domestic political standing. He did not seem to have a vision or a concept for conducting the nation's foreign policy. I believed that, with the past as my guide, a Republican would do a better job. Some of my closest colleagues at the Agency thought I was a bit nuts in my desire to see a change in the White House, but I told them that I wanted to work for an administration that took foreign policy seriously.

The Clinton team was a collection of intelligent amateurs who looked at foreign policy as a boutique item, an object of curiosity, not as an urgent matter of national security. In the last year of Clinton's term, I went to a meeting of the National Security Council with another analyst who was helping it roll out its critique of Saddam's human rights violations. The analyst had put a lot of work into her white paper, and the session was supposed to get everyone prepared for an announcement by the State Department. Then, nothing. Finally, the State Department held a press conference to release the white paper detailing Saddam's human rights violations. Trouble was, the press conference coincided with a political primary, and Saddam was lost on the inside pages of the newspapers. Next time, the State Department promised, it would check to see if there were other major news events happening that day.

Then, of course, there was the infamous Ohio town hall meeting where members of Clinton's principal national security team (Secretary of State Madeleine Albright, Secretary of Defense William Cohen, and National Security Adviser Sandy Berger) were shouted down and heckled by crowds as they tried to explain U.S. policy toward Iraq. A few more years of a Clinton-like president and Saddam might very well have gotten out from under international sanctions, which had already been weakening by the time Clinton left office.

My hopes for Bush were high because I recognized how well his father had handled foreign policy during his presidency. There was a real yearning at the CIA for a president who knew something about foreign policy and who would conduct the nation's statecraft with sophistication and care. The Clinton administration had placed domestic affairs above all else. I thought that George W. Bush would want to come into office and put an end to Saddam's flouting of international law, his potential to throw the Persian Gulf into chaos with another act of aggression, and his increasingly successful efforts to erode sanctions. But I also thought his administration's foreign policy would be deliberate, not impulsive. I assumed that Colin Powell would be a strong moderating influence. I assumed that Condoleezza Rice would be a brainy and independent national security adviser. And I assumed that Dick Cheney would return to the form that had made him such a successful secretary of defense. Well, Rice was smart but weak, Powell was marginalized by administration neocons, and Cheney was even more effective than he had been at the Defense Department, but in a darker way.

After Bush won the recount, many people at the CIA hoped he would name a director who would bring back the kind of stewardship his father practiced when he led the Agency in the 1970s. But the father had a much more nuanced feel for the intelligence business than the son did. The elder Bush understood the many shades of gray that went into analysis and assessment. He knew that there were few whole truths in intelligence, and that sometimes conclusions were just based on a long line of hunches. He also appreciated the dividing line between analysis and policy, and he took care not to drag the Agency across that line. Most important, Bush 41 understood what role the CIA director should play. In his book *A World Transformed*, which he wrote with his national security adviser Brent Scowcroft after leaving the presidency, the elder Bush laid out his vision of how the director of Central Intelligence (DCI) should do his job:

> He is not, and should not be, a policymaker or implementer, and should remain above politics, dealing solely with intelligence. The only exception to that role, I strongly feel, concerned covert action as part of a specific policy decision. I never asked to be accorded cabinet rank and I felt strongly that the DCI should not even attend cabinet meetings unless they related to foreign and national security policy.

After 9/11, George W. Bush told the world that they were either with us or against us. Many experts thought this Manichean worldview was a product of the terrorist attacks. In fact, it was the way Bush viewed everything. The same "us versus them" ethos pervaded the Bush administration even before 9/11, after his narrow victory over Gore. Officials associated with the Clinton administration were the enemy. They had been against him and were to be moved out. Fair enough, because that's usually how our political system works.

There was one big exception: Clinton's CIA director, George Tenet, wanted to stay in his job and went to great lengths to show how much he could help the Bush team when it came to foreign policy and national security. As Bush wrote in his 2010 memoir, *Decision Points*:

> With Rumsfeld going to the Pentagon, I no longer had a leading candidate for the CIA. I had great respect for the

Agency as a result of Dad's time there. I had been receiving intelligence briefings as president-elect for a few weeks when I met the sitting director, George Tenet. He was the opposite of the stereotypical CIA director you read about in spy novels, the bow-tied, Ivy League, elite type. Tenet was a blue-collar guy, the son of Greek immigrants from New York City. He spoke bluntly, often colorfully, and obviously cared deeply about the Agency.

It was indicative of Bush's callowness that he imagined the stereotypical CIA director as effete and elitist, a liberal wearing a bow tie who did not understand the administration's tough-guy view of the world. While he offered a disclaimer that this characterization was the stuff of spy novels, it really was the way that he and most of his administration viewed the CIA. The irony is that Bush was enormously proud of his father and his stewardship at the CIA, and yet the elder Bush (like his son) was the ultimate elitist, a product of Andover, Yale, and Skull and Bones. But the new president wanted a rough-hewn guy, a man's man, to lead his CIA. In reality, he wanted a patsy, someone he could control. Cheney and Rumsfeld also wanted a compliant director who would play dead if anything went wrong. They found the ideal chief in George Tenet, whose overweening ambition to be a downtown player set the stage for his own failure.

That said, Tenet did many things at the CIA that were good. He saw that the Agency was demoralized in the 1990s after a series of setbacks (the Aldrich Ames arrest for espionage, rumors of CIA involvement in the spread of crack cocaine in the

United States, and budget cuts implemented by the Clinton administration). Tenet tried to restore morale during the Clinton years and was partly successful. He was able to increase the Agency's budget, and he kick-started the recruiting process. But Tenet was too eager to please the White House. He encouraged analysts to punch up their reports even when the evidence was flimsy, and he surrounded himself with yes men. Most disturbing was how Tenet got played by the administration. He wanted intelligence that would be a hit downtown. He always aspired to be one of the big boys at the White House. What he didn't know was that the Bush administration, particularly the neocons around the vice president, had little respect for the CIA and would be only too happy to make the Agency the scapegoat if anything went wrong in Iraq.

During the end of the Clinton years, we were constantly being told that we had to do "opportunity analysis"—that we couldn't be satisfied telling policymakers just the "what" and the "so what" of an issue. While this may seem to contradict the service approach to supporting the administration's intelligence needs, it really doesn't. Not when you have an intelligence agency that does all that it can to ingratiate itself with an administration and reassure policymakers that it can take care of any and all needs. Somewhere between my EOD date in 1998 and the war in Iraq, CIA analysis evolved from "Dare to be wrong" to "Let the policymakers decide what they want and give them what they ask for, to the best of our abilities." It seems that by 2005 at the latest, the Agency leadership had caught on to a phenomenon that is quite typical in many other governments:

When an administration has failed spectacularly, as it had on 9/11 and in the Iraq War, the intelligence and the intelligence agencies must carry the blame for public consumption.

By 1999, analysts were asked more and more to tell policymakers what options they had—which, in my view, skirted closer to the edge of prescribing policy. As Tenet's protégé and my former boss Phil told us, "They are too busy to know what is going on. Therefore we have to help them come up with the solution." This was important to Phil because he intended to drive the point home to his superiors on the seventh floor that he was providing valuable answers for policymakers, namely what to do about Saddam. The seventh floor at Langley wanted to show their relevance to the new crowd. When I came to the Agency, three years before the Bush administration took office, it was drummed into me that we should not be making policy. But now we were told that we needed to be part of the mix downtown, and that the survival of the Agency depended on it.

Iraq intelligence became highly politicized during the Bush years. The new president did not have a sophisticated understanding of Islamic issues or the intelligence process. In Crawford, Texas, in 2000, while he waited for the Supreme Court to decide the presidential election, Bush continued to get briefings from the CIA, as he had throughout the campaign. One day during the recount, he told the briefer that he couldn't wait for the election to be decided. The briefer thought this was a natural reaction to the anxiety of waiting to see who won the cliffhanger contest. Then Bush added, "I can't wait, so that I can start seeing the real secret stuff you guys have." He thought the CIA was withholding sensitive intelligence until a winner was decided. Bush did not believe he was privy to the same top-secret information that Al Gore was receiving. This caused a few chuckles back at Langley. Soon, though, the president's naiveté would become a serious issue and no one would be laughing.

Shortly after Bush became president, a senior analyst went to the Oval Office to give him a tutorial on Islam. When told there was a Sunni-Shia schism based on divergent beliefs over who should be the heir to the mantle of the Prophet Muhammad, the president responded, "Wait. I thought you said they were all Muslims?" If ever there was a moment when we should have been trying to educate the president about the Middle East, this was it. Instead, Tenet and his aides on the seventh floor chose to cater to his ignorance by giving the boss what he wanted—more "opportunity analysis" that would help the president define how to best deal with Saddam Hussein.

I think Bush's attempts to get the CIA to support his political aims stemmed from his relationship with his father. The son always walked in the shadow of his father. When he went into politics and won political office in his own right, he could point to the fact that he was elected to an office that his father never held, governor of Texas. After he became president, Bush was not satisfied with merely disagreeing with or distrusting the CIA, as many of the people in his administration did. He wanted the Agency to rally behind his desire to go to war against Saddam Hussein. Bush 43 was determined to outdo Bush 41. It was almost like watching a test of strength. Whether compelling Saddam to surrender or forcing the CIA to support his efforts,

Bush wanted to prove that he was a more powerful chief executive than his father had been.

The issue of Saddam and what to do about him went into hyperdrive after the 9/11 attacks. The very next day, according to White House adviser Richard Clarke, Bush asked Clarke to find the links between Saddam and the attacks. Undersecretary of Defense Paul Wolfowitz wanted to know how many times Saddam had threatened the United States in speeches or comments made to the media. The CIA was asked to look through its files and find any connections to terrorism. Everything the Iraqi dictator had ever done was now given renewed scrutiny. It was clear in Langley that the White House would look with favor on interpretations that supported its desire to solve the Iraq problem once and for all.

A good example of this was the handling of intelligence provided by Ahmad Chalabi's Iraqi National Congress. The group was notorious for supplying self-serving information. The material from the Iraqi National Congress wasn't vetted and evaluated. Instead it was funneled to the Pentagon and used to justify the war. Responsible CIA analysts refused to endorse the interpretations by hard-liners in the intelligence community and administration "experts" downtown. The issue came to a head when the Counterterrorism Center (CTC) wrote a paper on ties between Saddam's government and international terrorism. This was one of the most controversial reports circulated by an office in the Directorate of Intelligence during the run-up to war. It was full of holes, inaccuracies, sloppy reporting, and pie-in-the-sky analysis. What made it worse was that the CTC believed the evidence. Iraq Issue was given three hours to review the paper before it was disseminated to the White House. To its great credit, Iraq Issue refused to concur with the analysis and drafted a long dissenting note that detailed its numerous errors. This dissenting note was transmitted to the seventh floor, where it was gutted by Deputy Director Jami Miscik and then given to Tenet to bring downtown. Much of this reporting was used by Defense Department hard-liners such as Douglas Feith to justify the invasion of Iraq.

As it became clear that the White House was gearing up for war against Iraq, the CIA lined up behind the president, reassigning analysts from other divisions to the Iraq office. Many of them had spent years working on the Balkan wars of the 1990s and were careerists looking for a new horse to ride in the race for promotions. Also during this time, the National Clandestine Service decided to cover its flanks by reviewing unreleased material and putting all reporting that had anything to do with Iraq or terrorism into official channels. Much of this material had been held back because of serious questions about its validity.

The dissemination of reams of spotty reporting undermined the credibility of the Iraq desk. Suddenly, the intelligence community had a plethora of instant Iraq "experts" and massive amounts of old material, much of it sensational, to reevaluate. This produced a perfect storm of shoddy analysis. Discarded reporting was suddenly presented as solid intelligence. The era of analytic mediocrity had begun, and Iraq was its first casualty. It made the CIA complicit in the tragedy of Iraq.

"I decided early on that I would not criticize the hardworking patriots of the CIA for the faulty intelligence on Iraq," Bush later wrote. "I did not want to repeat the nasty finger-pointing investigations that devastated the intelligence community in the 1970s." But that is exactly what he did. He gutted the Agency, blamed it for everything that went wrong in Iraq, and called its analysis "guesswork." He had heard only what he wanted to hear.

13.

The First Draft of History

- - - - - - - - - -

The proverbial first draft of history comes from the journalists who cover a major event. The second phase comes from the participants who race to get their versions out while they are still big names and publishers are writing big checks.

As the memoirs began to appear, I was struck by how off the mark most of them were. Naturally I was most interested in the hunt for Saddam and his debriefing. I was shocked to see how much intelligence supplied by the CIA, both from the field and from headquarters, was simply ignored. The senior political players held tight to their justifications for going to war, even when the facts showed they had been mistaken. They were like survivors of a shipwreck clinging to life rafts.

This was partly a reflection of the disconnect between Washington and the field, which grew wider as the war progressed. Sometimes the brass in Washington got stirred up by a rumor that agents in the field knew was a figment of some crackpot's imagination. I was gobsmacked when I read in Bush's *Decision Points* about Saddam's supposed plot to kill his daughters. Despite all evidence to the contrary, he still believed that his daughters were in Saddam's crosshairs. But nowhere does Bush mention his meeting with the emir of Bahrain in 2002, when the president said Saddam had tried to kill his father and that was the reason why he was going after him.

When I finished reading Bush's memoir, I came away further convinced that he had learned nothing about Iraq or Saddam Hussein. Bush's book was a defense of his belief that Saddam was a threat to the United States, even after the invasion and multiple interrogations made clear that Saddam was a paper tiger as far as America was concerned. Bush wrote about a National Security Council meeting on March 19, 2003, in which he asked his military commanders if victory could be achieved. The world's superpower against a third-rate military? How could anyone answer in the negative? But no one asked Bush if victory would be worth the cost in blood, treasure, and regional stability. The senior leadership knew Bush had already made up his mind. And rare is the time when a subordinate is willing to tell the president of the United States, "Sir, you are making a mistake."

One of the most troubling aspects of Bush's memoir was his depiction of Saddam Hussein on the eve of war. "There was one person with the power to avoid war, and he chose not to use it. For all his deception of the world, the person Saddam ultimately deceived the most was himself," Bush wrote. This showed a fundamental misreading of who Saddam was and why he did the things he did. Saddam was ready to negotiate. During the Clinton and George W. Bush years, Saddam said that he was ready to talk to the United States at any time. He said so on many occasions, both before and after his capture.

In the months before the invasion, friends of mine would come back from National Security Council meetings and recount the fantastical logic of the Bush White House. The Bush team wanted nothing to do with anyone linked to Saddam or the Ba'ath Party. This was downright scary. They were about to order the invasion of a country without the slightest clue about the people they would be attacking. Even after Saddam's capture, the White House was only looking for information that supported its decision to go to war. (In the run-up to the invasion, I wondered how long it would be before the administration turned its gaze to Iran, the country I was studying at the time. In fact, administration officials did consider moving against Iran, but Iraq proved so intractable that they were never able to take any action in Iran. As much as I loathed the leadership in Tehran, it was a blessing that the Bush team didn't try regime change there.)

In his memoir, *Known and Unknown*, Donald Rumsfeld also implicitly blamed Saddam for not avoiding war. He wrote that the administration hoped that "an aggressive diplomatic effort, coupled by a threat of military force, just might convince Saddam and those around him to seek exile . . . If there were enough rational individuals around Saddam, they might be convinced that George W. Bush was not bluffing and was committed to the disarmament of Saddam Hussein."

Rumsfeld was suggesting that Saddam's lackeys might be able to convince him to leave the country to avert war, basically to surrender. This was another profound misreading of the Iraqi leader. Saddam was immensely proud of his roots, had traveled abroad only twice, and almost certainly would never leave Iraq—for any reason. Iraq was more than his country; it was his entire identity. This message was often conveyed to Washington policymakers. Were they listening? Was Rumsfeld listening? I can conclude only that U.S. policymakers were prisoners of what they thought they knew before the war started, countervailing intelligence be damned.

When he was promoting his book, President Bush went on *Oprah* and implausibly claimed he hadn't wanted to go to war. In a similar vein, Rumsfeld wrote that Bush was *not* intent on "fixing" Iraq once he came into office. Rumsfeld chided the Clinton administration for fecklessly appeasing Saddam but also said Iraq did not come up when he met with Bush in Austin before the inauguration. Yet it was clear in Bush's CIA briefings during the transition that Iraq was very much on his mind.

Rumsfeld said he wrote a memo to the president that offered three possible options for dealing with Saddam: (1) acknowledge that sanctions weren't working, (2) adopt a more assertive policy in conjunction with Saddam's Arab neighbors, or (3) try to initiate contact with Saddam to start a new chapter in U.S.–Iraq relations. I'm in no position to judge Rumsfeld's uppermost feelings. But I can say this: From all that I was able to glean from people close to him, Rumsfeld was not the reflexive hawk he was made out to be. He was not the person saying that we had to overthrow Saddam and go to war with Iraq. However, his poor relations with the military and his inadequate war plan contributed mightily to the Iraq failure. After the invasion, Rumsfeld impugned his earlier memo by claiming that Saddam applauded 9/11 and had ties with terrorists. He was wrong on both counts.

Rumsfeld also wrote that the White House believed that Saddam was paying his agents $60 million to assassinate his own daughters as well as Bush's girls. This was ludicrous, because Saddam was in hiding and could barely get good reception on his radio, which Rumsfeld surely knew. To make matters worse, Rumsfeld quoted George Tenet as saying, "You took out Saddam's sons. They might well go after your daughters." Tenet, evidently to please his masters, completely misrepresented what his agents in the field had told him. The author Ron Suskind called this the "one percent solution," on the basis of a remark he attributed to Cheney. According to this proposition, even if there's only a 1 percent chance of intelligence reporting being correct, the administration should treat it as fully vetted and true.

Rumsfeld also raised the old chestnut of Saddam's body double. Of all the enduring myths of Saddam's rule, none was so durable as that of the body double. No matter how many times intelligence analysts knocked down the notion, it seemed impossible to disabuse Bush, Rumsfeld, and other policymakers. The Bush team simply dismissed out of hand anything that cast doubt on it. Even worse, as the war progressed and as Iraq became a blame game between who was right and who was wrong, the administration's belief in body doubles seemed to grow. The Bush administration was convinced it was right, no matter what the intelligence showed.

Rumsfeld went so far as to depict Paul Bremer, administrator of the Coalition Provisional Authority, as a rogue bureaucrat run amok in Mesopotamia—even though he and Cheney gave Bremer his marching orders every day. They told him to proceed with de-Ba'athification and to disband the Iraqi army. But in his memoir, Rumsfeld blamed Bremer for delaying the transfer of sovereignty to the Iraqis.

Such historical make-believe was not reserved for this side of the Atlantic. British prime minister Tony Blair's memoir was as stubbornly defensive as Bush's. I had hoped that Blair, a more worldly man than Bush, would have the courage to admit that Britain had participated in the invasion under assumptions that proved mistaken. Instead, Blair went on at length about the gathering threat that Saddam posed. He cited the work of the Duelfer commission on weapons of mass destruction and said that Saddam "retained completely his belief in the strategic importance of WMD to his regime and its survival. He believed that the use of chemical weapons had been vital in repelling the Iranian soldiers who, filled with religious zeal, had thrown themselves in waves against Iraqi forces in the Iran-Iraq War. Only their use had, he thought, compensated for the superior numbers of Iran's forces . . . For him, the acquisition of such nuclear capability would serve his basic purpose: to be the dominant force in the Arab world."

Nowhere in the interrogations of Saddam, his political and military aides, and his top scientists was there any evidence supporting Blair's assertion that Iraq threatened its neighbors, much less the West, with chemical weapons or, more outlandishly, with nuclear arms. If anything, the evidence pointed in the opposite direction. Yes, chemical weapons had played a decisive role in the war against Iran, but Saddam had destroyed his WMD before the 2003 invasion. As for nuclear weapons, Saddam may have dreamed of acquiring them, but he never admitted as much and he certainly never came close to getting them.

One of the great ironies of the Iraq War was that brutal dictator Saddam Hussein and freedom fighter George W. Bush were alike in many ways. Both had haughty, imperious demeanors. Both were fairly ignorant of the outside world and had rarely traveled abroad. Both tended to see things as black and white, good and bad, or for and against, and became uncomfortable when presented with multiple alternatives. Both surrounded themselves with compliant advisers and had little tolerance for dissent. Both prized unanimity, at least when it coalesced behind their own views. Both distrusted expert opinion. The similarities go on:

- Both had little meaningful military experience and had unrealistic expectations about what force could achieve.
- Both made military decisions based on political objectives. Both failed to understand that the judicious use of power, or even the threat of power, can be more effective than brute force. Both took countries that were enjoying peace and prosperity and drove them into war and debt.
- Both men rose to preeminence by strictly adhering to their political philosophies. However, by the end of their

respective careers, both were willing to jettison ideological positions in favor of more pragmatic policies. Both had highly developed political skills and an ability to project warmth to large audiences. But both were cool and aloof in person, although they could turn on the charm when it suited their purposes.

- Both considered themselves great men and were determined that history see them that way.

- Both confessed to me that they were "gut players," politicians who trusted their instincts more than their intellect.

- Both were isolated from reality during their years in power. While Baghdad was about to fall, Saddam was sending off proofs of a novel he had written. In an interview shortly before he left the White House, Bush said he enjoyed being in the bubble, the cocoonlike existence of the Oval Office that insulates the occupant from the outside world.

- Both were risk takers, a trait that served them well when scaling the heights of power but proved to be their Achilles' heels once they got to the top. Both rolled the dice in taking their countries to war. Saddam invaded Iran and Kuwait, and Bush invaded Afghanistan and Iraq.

One could argue that Bush was right to attack Afghanistan after 9/11, but his decision to invade Iraq was based on false premises and didn't serve American interests. Bush, Cheney, and Rumsfeld did their best to justify the war in their memoirs, but no serious Middle East analyst believes that Saddam Hussein was a threat to the United States.

Bush came out to CIA headquarters near the end of his presidency to "thank" us for our hard work, never mind that he had thrown the CIA under the bus several times. He gave a typically disjointed speech. He trotted out all his familiar red-meat lines, but put the emphasis on the wrong words, robbing the talk of its punch. Everyone with him just smiled. CIA chief Mike Hayden basked in the glow. Stephen Hadley worked on his cell phone, something that for the rest of us would have been a serious security violation. And then there was the president, talking about how the future belonged to freedom. "Don't let anyone tell you anything else. There is a God and He believes in freedom!" he told his audience. "There are those who would argue that it is OK for some people to live under dictators. That it's just too bad and that it's tough luck for you if you have to live in one of these societies." Strangely enough, Bush looked at me when he made his next point: "Don't listen to those people. Those people are *eeeeeeLEETeests,*" he said, dragging out the word for effect. Once again I was struck that these words were coming from a man shaped by Andover, Yale, and Skull and Bones.

No one knew quite what to expect from the incoming Obama administration in 2009. Most people I worked with were glad to see him elected. I was too. I thought that he would have the cast of mind to understand the finer points of foreign policy. My boss had been his briefer on the campaign trail, and he said that the president-elect was deliberate and analytic, an avid reader who was a sponge for information. This was good news, especially in light of what we had heard about the McCain and Palin team. John McCain reportedly was a screamer and pretty rough on staff. While he had a lot more foreign policy expertise than Obama did, McCain was another shoot-from-the-hip kind of politician. I thought we'd had enough of that with Bush. As for Sarah Palin, my goodness, where would one begin?

We thought that Iraq would be on Obama's daily list of foreign policy priorities. Before Bush left office, he asked my office to prepare several studies on key issues in Iraq for "the new guy." We complied with his wishes and were prepared to help the new team get up to speed. And then we waited. And waited. And waited some more. Soon it became clear that the Obama White House really didn't want much to do with Iraq. During the Bush administration, the Iraq office sent analysts to the Oval Office on a weekly basis. Now we had no access to the president other than memos that might wind up in his daily intelligence briefing. Obama apparently did not see Iraq as his problem and apparently had no intention of investing the time, effort, and political capital needed to continue with a policy that he inherited from the Bush administration. This was deeply unfortunate because the Obama White House tuned out just as we were making progress in tamping down the violence in Iraq.

I left the Iraq desk in 2009, but I kept in touch with friends who continued to work there and also stayed abreast of developments in the region. In the first two years of Obama's presidency, the White House asked for only one deep-dive briefing on Iraq. The administration was simply not interested, or acted like it wasn't. It showed in little ways at first. It became increasingly difficult to get a memo on Iraq into the daily briefing book. Then CIA budgets for Iraq analysis were cut, and the legions of analysts who had come to Iraq Issue between 2004 and 2006 began to work on Afghanistan, a place the Obama administration was paying attention to.

The beginning of any administration is always a tricky time for the CIA. The Agency does all it can to prove its value to the new president, feeling out the administration about its priorities and offering to help in any way it can. Often the Agency can be of great assistance. Occasionally it oversells itself. And sometimes it finds itself face to face with a very skeptical client. This was the case with Obama. The new president could not understand why the government spent so much on intelligence but, in his view, got so little in return.

The decline of Iraq's importance at the White House was soon felt in Baghdad. In 2009, the administration passed over General Anthony Zinni, a former CENTCOM commander, for ambassador to Iraq and instead picked Christopher Hill, a State Department careerist who had served as special envoy to North Korea during the Bush years and had worked on the Balkans during the Clinton years. Zinni had been promised the slot by Vice President Biden and the Obama transition team. Ambassador Ryan Crocker, Hill's predecessor, had hoped that the Baghdad post would go to either William Burns or Beth Jones, two seasoned diplomats who would have been perfect for the role. However, the new secretary of state, Hillary Clinton, objected to two former generals' serving in such sensitive posts in both Iraq and Afghanistan (former general Karl Eikenberry was the ambassador in Kabul). Clinton probably feared that she would have trouble controlling a person like Zinni because he had much more experience in the region than she did. Also, Hill was a protégé of Richard Holbrooke, who was very close to Secretary Clinton and served under her as the adviser on Afghanistan and Pakistan at the State Department. Holbrook may have reasoned that the more people he could place near his area of responsibility, the easier his job would be. However, Hill was a disastrous choice. He had no knowledge of the region and didn't seem to think any was required. An analyst gave him a paper I had written about Muqtada al-Sadr and his family, and Hill's response was, "Do I need to know this?" He did not speak the language, did not know the history of Iraq, and did not know any of the players on the Iraqi side whom he needed to know to be effective in his job. He was out of his depth and seemed to be waiting for his chance to leave the Middle East. Thus started the downward spiral of U.S. policy in Iraq, paid for in thousands of lives and trillions of dollars.

More important, the Maliki government was moving in a decidedly more sectarian direction. It is worth remembering that Maliki became prime minister during the worst of the fighting between Baghdad and the al-Qaeda in Iraq insurgency (2004–7), which was founded by Zarqawi and eventually morphed into ISIS. Maliki was a compromise choice after the U.S. government lost confidence in Ibrahim al-Jaafari, who had been elected prime minister in 2005 but was forced to quit in 2006. Maliki got off to a slow start and told *The Wall Street Journal* that he disliked the job and couldn't wait for his term to be over. However, the execution of Saddam at the end of 2006 seemed to bring about a change in his attitude. Maliki began to emerge as more of a leader in his own right.

After the surge of U.S. troops in 2007, coupled with the Sunni tribal "Awakening," when many of the Sunni tribes in Anbar province switched sides to join with the Americans to fight al-Qaeda in Iraq, Maliki stopped talking about relinquishing power. Quite the opposite. The next big step for Maliki came during the 2008 Charge of the Knights campaign, when he took on the Shia militias in Baghdad and southern Iraq. This was around the time when Bush thought that Maliki had dealt a death blow to Muqtada al-Sadr. He hadn't. In fact, if it hadn't been for the intervention of U.S. forces in Basra, Maliki might have found himself taken prisoner by the Sadrists. (Maliki had gone to Basra to supervise the operation and came close to having his command center surrounded by the militias.)

A key turning point in the post-surge U.S.–Iraqi relationship came during the 2011 Iraqi election. Maliki and his State of Law coalition had been expected to win but were outpolled by his Shia rival Ayad Allawi. A favorite of the U.S. government—especially of the CIA—and a secular Shia who had good ties to the Sunni community, Allawi narrowly defeated Maliki and was eager to form a new government.

At this point the Obama government made a strategic mistake that had powerful reverberations in Iraq. The longer Maliki served in office, the more authoritarian he became. Americans and Iraqis alike began to comment on the new Maliki, the one who was acting more like Saddam. During the campaign, Maliki began to reach out to Shia tribes for support. Maliki shared state largesse with the larger tribes in an effort to undercut Allawi. Maliki also gained the support of the Marja'iyah, or Shia religious leadership, in Najaf. This effort to use religious and tribal support to build a foundation of power was, whether intentional or not, directly analogous to how Saddam ran Iraq. Maliki also had been for some time accruing greater power and authority for the office of the prime minister. He increased his grip by creating the Office of the Commander in Chief to circumvent the army's chain of command and by creating provincial command centers that allowed him to control the elite Iraqi Security Forces.

Maliki insisted that the 2011 election had been rigged. This was the moment when the Obama administration should have stepped in and told him it was time to go. This would have confirmed the legitimacy of the election and given the Iraqis another peaceful handover of power. Instead, the Obama administration chose the path of least resistance. It said that Maliki was America's man and that it would be better for U.S. interests if he served a second term.* Unfortunately, the Iraq portfolio in the Obama administration always seemed to be in the hands of Vice President Biden, whose grasp of foreign policy seemed shaky at best. His major contribution to the Iraq debate during his years in the Senate was to suggest that Iraq would benefit by being broken into three parts: Sunnistan, Kurdistan, and Shiastan. No expert took this seriously.

In 2010, Biden reportedly told others in the administration that he would bet his vice presidency on Maliki's willingness to renew the Status of Forces Agreement (SOFA) between the United States and Iraq, which gave U.S. forces the right to re-

---

*Ali Khedery, "Why We Stuck with Maliki—and Lost Iraq," *The Washington Post*, July 3, 2014.

main in Iraq. Without the SOFA, the United States would have to pull out all its troops. No Iraqi politician wanted to go on record saying that they wanted to renew the SOFA, but almost all Iraqi politicians were fearful of what might happen if the U.S. military left Iraq. In the end, the SOFA died and Iraq was truly sovereign again, with all that entailed. The worst consequence of the SOFA's demise was the renewed sectarianism of the Maliki government. He began to persecute his Sunni rivals, which resulted in the raid on the office and home of Minister of Finance Rafi al-Issawi, and issued a death sentence against Vice President Tariq al-Hashemi. This sparked renewed protests in Anbar Province in late 2013. Sunni insurgents who had been operating under a succession of names soon marched under the flag of ISIS, committing atrocities that would have made Zarqawi proud.

14.

Leaving with Regrets

By 2009, I had been to Iraq eight times. Some trips lasted several months, others only four to six weeks. I had done analytic work there on sectarian tensions and Iraq's relations with its neighbors. I did two stints filling in for the U.S. ambassador's regular briefer, and I participated in the hunt for Zarqawi. On my final trip, which lasted only a week, I exchanged information with other intelligence operatives. I was one of the more senior analysts on the trip. I flew to Baghdad with a number of analysts and several representatives from the CIA's seventh floor. I couldn't get over how much our compound had changed. It was like a ghost town. I also could not get over how quiet things were. During the entire week I did not hear a single bomb or explosion.

My last long stay in Iraq was in 2006. I was part of a strategic issues group doing field research to answer a particular policymaker's question (the CIA prevents me from saying what the subject was). My teammates in this effort were Ben T., Eric B., and Elisa S. They were great colleagues, and we did some fine work for the Agency and managed to enjoy ourselves by doing our work without the constraints of being at CIA headquarters. Being in Iraq as an analyst meant you had autonomy. You could dress as you liked, and you could walk to work because the office was just yards from your trailer. You were paid more for working in a war zone. You were not tied to the whims of your managers at headquarters, and you were not buried under the production schedule that required you to be writing current intelligence every week. From the field, you were able to gain some ground truth as to what was going on in Iraq, and that was better than sitting in your cubicle listing cables for a memo that might or might not be read. Ben and Eric were analysts who brought a lot of depth to the job at hand. Elisa coordinated our schedules so that we could get around with a minimum of fuss—not an easy task. The summer was relatively quiet, and we were all sched-uled to leave in early September. But it turned out that I would have one more disquieting interlude before I could leave the be-nighted country. In August, the Israel-Hezbollah War broke out. As soon as Israel began shelling Beirut, the Sadrists began shelling Baghdad's Green Zone in a sympathy attack. We had always known that Sadr had a special admiration for Hasan Nasrallah, and now we found ourselves scurrying daily for pro-tection from mortars and rockets. I couldn't wait to get out of there.

When I returned to the States in 2006 after this nine-month tour, I had a chunk of holiday coming because of the time I had spent in a war zone. I went to California to visit my family and stayed for almost three weeks. On the day I was due to go back to Washington, I was struck by a sense of dread about being desk-bound in Langley again. On my way to the airport I tried to figure out an excuse for not getting on the plane. My gut was telling me that it was time to leave the Agency. But if I had quit then, I would have missed my chance to tell the president and the vice president what I had seen and what I knew.

Back in Langley, I started thinking about an analytic assignment that would take me away from Iraq. I was simply burned out on the place. The final straw came when I wrote a long paper on Muqtada al-Sadr and his followers. I concluded that they would be a force to be reckoned with in Shia politics for the next five years. Sadr was the third rail in intelligence analysis. General Raymond Odierno, who was the commanding general in Baghdad at the time, read my paper and inelegantly replied, "You've got to be shitting me." Odierno seemed to be most upset by my analysis because it directly contradicted his own personal viewpoint and what he had been telling the president and the vice president about progress in Iraq. Once again I had to water down an analysis to please policymakers. All of a sudden, I was asked to write a paper on what Sadr would be like six months from now, not five years from now. I was paired with a new analyst and we worked together on revising the Sadr analysis. As usual, it took months to get the paper out the door, and it was merely a rehash of the paper that Odierno had criticized, but tailored to avoid his criticisms.

Moving to a new desk is somewhat traumatic for analysts who have worked on the same portfolio for a long time. You know you need a fresh challenge, but you're apprehensive about leaving your comfort zone. One day I saw an internal advertisement for a leadership analyst for North Korea. I thought maybe this would be just the thing I needed to get my intellectual juices flowing again. And let's face it, watching the crazy world of Kim Jong Il would be nothing if not entertaining. My friends thought I was crazy, but I interviewed for the job and soon agreed to join the North Korean team. It was an unusual career move because it took me out of the region that I was familiar with. However, North Korea was high on the White House's priority list, and it guaranteed me what I thought would be a fresh start on a highly relevant account.

I got to work on North Korea and Kim, but I couldn't get myself motivated. The Agency seemed completely locked into its interpretation of Kim, and every day did battle with the State Department over how we should view his regime. Worse still, Kim's regime was beginning to feel a lot like Saddam's. I said to myself, "Boy, I've been to this movie before, and I know it's not going to end well." I could also see that it would take me years before I was conversant on North Korea. I realized that I knew nothing about Asia, and I no longer had the desire to start from scratch on a subject and patiently educate myself. I was aware of the irony of reversing the journey that Christopher Hill had taken from Korea to Iraq. But he was an ambassador who could call on experts for guidance. I was an analyst and was expected to be an expert myself. My only option, I concluded, was to leave the CIA after thirteen years.

In one sense, leaving was a liberating experience. (I moved to a sister agency, the National Counterterrorism Center in McLean, Virginia.) So many people at the CIA get hooked into life there and can't imagine how they will function on the outside. Either they don't want to give up their access to "secret" information, or they don't want to leave until they have put in the years they need to retire, or they just like doing government work. For whatever reason, many people choose to stay, even after their work becomes humdrum. I was leaving precisely because my work no longer excited me. There was nothing left for me to do but chase promotions.

For me, the best part of working for the Agency was the opportunity to do things I couldn't do anywhere else. When it lost that, it lost everything. It had become clear to me that the CIA had become a sclerotic organization, despite all the young blood it had brought in over the past few years. The Agency still thought it could take anyone and make him or her a first-rate analyst within a few months. I can say from hard experience that this approach simply doesn't work. What may be worse was that the CIA lagged far behind technologically in certain areas of analytic research. It took so long to get new research technology approved for purchase that it was often obsolete by the time it was deployed. This was part of a hidebound mind-set that prevented analysts from doing their best work. After I left the Agency, the Directorate of Intelligence, the DI, changed its name to the Directorate of Analysis, the DA. The Agency is very good at changing names, but not very good at changing its ethos and its methods.

I had played a very small part in a very large disaster in American foreign policy: the Iraq War. My CIA colleagues and I finished our work with deep regret for what had happened to America's image in the world, for all the U.S. men and women who were killed in action or came home with physical and/or mental wounds, and for what the United States inflicted on the people of Iraq. On my first day in Iraq in October 2003, the person driving me from the airport to ██████ near the Republican Palace saw a group of children playing by the side of the road and said, "That is why we're here." I remember thinking, "I hope so," but wondering whether he was right.

Since then, I have come to see that his hopes were misplaced. We were there because of neocon fantasies about bringing the region under American suzerainty and because of President Bush's misguided belief that Saddam had tried to kill his father. Was Saddam worth removing from power? I can speak only for myself when I say that the answer must be no. Saddam was busy writing novels in 2003. He was no longer running the government. Would his sons have been able to succeed him? Possibly, but they might not have lasted for long. More likely, someone from the Sunni military-security axis would have grabbed power through a coup. It wouldn't have been pretty, but at least it would have been an Iraqi solution to the question of "Who leads Iraq?" The United States then could have reengaged with the new regime.

As of this writing, I can see only negative consequences for the United States from Saddam's overthrow. First, the Middle East has grown dependent on America to right the wrongs that plague the region and to serve as arbiter in local disputes. Nowhere was this more apparent than in Iraq. Every time the United States tried to get the Iraqis to reconcile their differences and rebuild their country, the Iraqi political class split along sectarian lines and vied for American support. Second, we spent trillions of dollars and wasted the lives of thousands of men and women in the military only to end up with a country that is infinitely more chaotic than Saddam's Ba'athist Iraq. Third, the genie of Islamic fundamentalism arose with a vengeance and poses a greater threat with each passing day. ISIS and al-Qaeda offshoots are proving to be more violent and harder to stamp out than the "core" al-Qaeda that masterminded 9/11 from its safe haven in Afghanistan.

The United States cannot allow the virulently anti-Western ISIS to hold territory that serves as a sanctuary and training ground for Islamic extremists. The jihadists are determined to snuff out Western influence in the region, inspire "lone wolf" attacks in the United States and Europe, and coordinate terrorist operations abroad with the goal of inflicting large numbers of civilian casualties, as happened in Paris in November 2015. The evolution of ISIS into a global terrorist organization, targeting both the "near enemy" of apostate regimes in the Middle East and the "far enemy" in the West, poses both a security threat and a dilemma over how to balance preventive measures and civil liberties. While it is too early to say whether the metastasis of ISIS poses a serious threat to the American homeland, we would do well to prepare for that dire possibility.

Iran appears to have been the big winner in the aftermath of our Iraq adventure. The Shiites in Tehran have seen the Sunni tyrant of Baghdad led to the gallows by their Iraqi Shia allies and now have a Shia-led government on their western border. (Iran has also benefited from the removal of the Taliban— another hostile neighbor—on its eastern border.) For the time being, at least, Iran no longer fears a militarized Iraq looking for a favorable conclusion to the stalemate that ended the eight-year war between the two nations. Iraq has become one of Tehran's largest trading partners. Indeed, the establishment of a Shia government in Baghdad has, whether rightly or wrongly, re-awakened fears that a "Shia Crescent" could one day dominate the region and threaten the Sunni monarchies.

The Kurds, who paid a bloody price for opposing Saddam's rule, may finally get their deliverance from Baghdad. Ostensibly led by Jalal Talabani's Patriotic Union of Kurdistan (PUK) and Masoud Barzani's Kurdish Democratic Party (KDP), the Kurds were often their own worst enemy. They fought against each other almost as much as they fought against Saddam. But after 9/11, they knew their ancient dream of an independent Kurdis-tan might finally be within reach.

The Shia political parties, mostly allied with Iran, were the biggest winners. At the same time, they have been the biggest opponents, along with the independence-minded Kurds, of sec-tarian and ethnic reconciliation in Iraq. Western democracies see political reconciliation as a panacea because it resolves the differences of various stakeholders. But this is not how Iraq works. Throughout the twentieth century and into the twenty-first, Iraqi politics has been a winner-take-all affair.

Former Bush administration officials like to point out that Saddam's fall triggered the Arab Spring. That may be true, but it's hardly something to brag about. The Arab Spring quickly turned into an Arab Winter of civil wars and political chaos. The failure of the Arab Spring showed, in some cases, the dura-bility of the Arab "deep state" of authoritarian leadership, and in others, the chaos that ensues when strong leadership is replaced with a power vacuum. Saddam's removal was a watershed event in the decline of the 1960s generation of Arab strongmen. However, his exit has left a vacuum that will likely be filled by strongmen with even bloodier hands.

The ouster of Saddam Hussein from power proved to be a calamity for Iraq. It is now a failed state, pure and simple. The debacle was caused by many factors: specious reasoning by the Bush administration to go to war, an invasion force that was far too small to both topple Saddam and maintain the peace after his fall, and the lack of a plan for a political transition after he was deposed. This political disaster does not entirely deserve a "Made in America" label. The United States had plenty of help from its Iraqi friends, the exiles who lobbied Washington for years to overthrow Saddam.

As hard as it is to say—and even harder for many to hear—we should not give up on Iraq. I saw up close what we tried to do to help Iraq, and I understand full well that we cannot do what the Iraqis won't do for themselves. But the United States must repair its ties with the Sunnis and do what it can to force the Shia-led government in Baghdad to be more tolerant and inclusive when dealing with their former rulers. This is a tall order, but it is necessary if Iraq and its neighbors are to defeat ISIS in the near or long term.

The CIA badly needs fixing, and I suspect the answer does not lie in Langley. The Bush years were tough. However, the Obama years have been tough as well. Obama never seemed to warm up to the Agency, and after he grew confident in his own vision of foreign policy, he had less and less interest in what the Agency had to say. The people who need to do the most soul-

searching about the uses of intelligence are the presidents themselves, along with policymakers in the executive branch and on
Capitol Hill. A good start would be to acknowledge that intelligence agencies can provide only information and insights, and
can't serve as a crystal ball to predict the future. The brass on the
seventh floor can do its part if they stop fostering the notion that
the CIA is omniscient.

CIA analysts must deepen their expertise. Right now the
trend at the CIA is to develop analytic tradecraft. This often
means developing assumptions and holding whiteboard sessions
at which everyone throws out ideas and criticisms. Using these
brainstorming sessions to test analytic viewpoints can be useful
if done correctly. But at present it's a false rigor. Such exercises
are mostly a cover-your-ass effort that headquarters can hold up
to tell its critics that it did everything it could to get the right
answer. The right answer comes when you have analysts with
depth, not when you have a large analytic cadre. The Agency's
paramount concern should be making sure its analysts have
enough expertise to offer facts worthy of a whiteboarding session. Otherwise the CIA will continue to fall victim to the computer trap: Garbage in, garbage out.

The CIA's cover-your-ass culture is a formidable obstacle.
Expertise is not valued, indeed not trusted, because experts can
be wrong. Look at Iran in 1978 and early 1979 when demonstrations and riots forced the shah to flee the country. The CIA had
a shocking lack of understanding of the opposition to the shah.
However, more often than not, greater expertise will help policymakers decide on a prudent course of action by giving them a

better understanding of the issues at play. For the last two and a
half years of Saddam's rule, the CIA did not have a good sense
of his regime. This was not because reporting had dried up. To
the contrary, reporting had exploded in a million directions.
What was seriously lacking was a real understanding of Saddam
and experienced analysts who could make sense of the reporting.

If we are to go to war again, as we surely will have to do
sooner or later, the United States has to make certain it's fighting for the right reasons. The conditions set forth by Colin Powell before the Gulf War should have served as criteria before we
decided on military action in 2003. The Powell Doctrine posed
a number of questions that must be answered affirmatively,
among them: Is a vital national security interest at stake? Have
the risks and costs been fully assessed? Have nonmilitary policies been exhausted? Do we have an exit strategy? Is military
action supported at home and abroad? Powell was marginalized
in the George W. Bush administration by White House aides
who were determined to finish off Saddam. His voice was ur-
gently missed.

The decision to get rid of Saddam ultimately rested with the
president, and it will be one of his enduring legacies. It appeared
to be motivated by highly personal reasons, and there seemed to
be very little thought given to what the United States would do
after the invasion—as if things would simply take care of themselves. Personalized policymaking comes from the heart, not the
head, and therefore often produces unwelcome consequences.
Iraq should serve as a cautionary tale for future presidents. It
should also have a sobering effect on the CIA, which was a will-

ing collaborator. The Agency slavishly sought to do the president's bidding—as it usually does—in an effort to get a seat near the center of power and justify its budget. That was the institutional imperative. But individuals at the Agency leaked like mad when they disagreed with presidential decisions related to the war. In my time at the Agency, I never saw so many leaks of critical and secret information, to the detriment of the administration, the Agency, and the armed forces.

Instead of demonizing foreign leaders, as it did with Saddam, the United States should approach them in a pragmatic and mature way. Democracies don't like strongmen, but sometimes authoritarian leaders help the United States deal with more nefarious actors, such as ISIS, al-Qaeda, and Iran. Once the United States starts down the road of demonizing its foreign opponents, for whatever reason, our options start constricting. In 1990, George H. W. Bush likened Saddam Hussein to Hitler. Maybe there was merit in the comparison, but the reality of it was that Bush then made it more difficult for himself and his successors to construct a creative policy toward Iraq. After all, who can negotiate with Hitler? Most of our political leaders have trouble understanding this concept. I know people will ask, "How can we have relations with people who murder their own?" But consider Syria. The effort to remove Bashar al-Assad has left hundreds of thousands dead and displaced half of Syria's population from their homes, creating a refugee crisis with grave consequences for the Middle East and Europe. It would be wonderful if there were a Syrian Thomas Jefferson waiting in the wings to take over from Assad after his fall, but no one has yet come forward to claim that mantle. This was the same message that we had to give to the Clinton and Bush administrations when we were asked about democratic alternatives to Saddam.

The United States must develop better intelligence capabilities, particularly human intelligence. The Iraq fiasco emphatically affirmed the need for people to collect information. Technical means—electronic intercepts and surveillance photos, among other things—are important, but they are bloodless instruments and need to be complemented with human beings who have a *feel* for how things are going on the ground.

In foreign affairs, the United States is constantly reinventing the wheel by quickly forgetting the lessons learned from the last war. Just as people forget pain, the United States develops a case of amnesia about the blood and treasure expended in a military conflict. We celebrate victories but don't hold the government fully accountable when the use of force does not achieve its objectives, or leaves chaos in its wake.

In the years since I left the CIA, I have often thought about Saddam. Hardly a day goes by when he doesn't skitter across my mind. Somehow he got under my skin and has stayed there. Perhaps it is because of the lasting guilt I feel for being associated with so much that went wrong in Iraq. When I first got back to the United States, I was asked how well we knew Saddam. I said I had gotten him pretty close to right. But years later, I realize that my colleagues and I didn't know him at all. We were locked into a perception of him based on the events of 1990–91, when he slaughtered hundreds of thousands of his own people in the turmoil that followed the Gulf War.

I saw Saddam up close every day for months, sparred with him over his brutal methods, debated history and leadership with him, experienced his charisma and the limits of his intelligence, respected him one day and hated him the next, and at the end came away with only an outline of the man. I will be filling in the blanks for the rest of my life.

A Hanging in the Middle
of the Night

It was December 2006, and I was put on Saddam execution watch at CIA headquarters in Langley. I was on call over the weekend and would report to the seventh floor if there were any developments. Because I had spent a lot of time with Saddam, I guess my boss thought I would be interested in his hanging. I wasn't. I didn't have any sympathy for Saddam, but the rush to execution had been unseemly. I had always thought his trial and punishment would be a highly choreographed affair, with a somber beginning, middle, and end. I was not prepared for what happened, and it shocked all of us who had followed his career.

Nuri al-Maliki's Shia government, in power at last, couldn't get rid of Saddam fast enough. The American government had beseeched the Iraqis to delay the execution because of Eid al-Adha, the Islamic holiday; the United States thought it would be an affront to the sensibilities of Muslims in Iraq and the region to hang Saddam so close to the holiday. As it happened, the

U.S. ambassador to Iraq, Zalmay Khalilzad, and his deputy, David Satterfield, were both out of the country for the Christmas holidays. Instructions were left at the embassy for the acting ambassador, Margaret Scobey, not to sign anything that would give a green light for the execution. Apparently both the State Department and the Department of Defense had to approve the transfer of Saddam from U.S. custody.

Saddam had often said that he was not afraid to die and seemed reconciled to his end. Death would probably be a relief for him. He had bridled at his confinement and the humiliations visited on him during his trial. (Abd al-Aziz al-Hakim, chief of the Supreme Council for the Islamic Revolution, a leading Shia political party, made a slicing motion across his throat when Saddam entered court for the first time.) A friend of mine in the embassy later told me, "All that Scobey had to do was do nothing. Her signature was required for the execution to proceed, and she had been given explicit orders from the ambassador and his deputy not to sign off on anything until they returned from the Christmas holidays in the States. And Scobey was good at doing nothing. But in this case, she buckled under pressure from the military, who wanted to unload Saddam onto the Iraqis and be rid of him once and for all." This is how some of the momentous occasions in history take place: not with great deliberation and forethought, but by chance and circumstance.

I thought Saddam's execution would be televised because it would show the world, especially the Iraqis, that he had died according to the rule of law. Instead, the exchange took place in the dark of night, after midnight, as a U.S. helicopter took Saddam from his prison to a compound where he was handed over to the Maliki government. Saddam was then whisked to a basement of an Iraqi ministry building by his captors. God knows what must have transpired between Saddam and his captors. What the world saw the next day was, in my opinion, shocking. On a cell phone video, Saddam was seen ascending a makeshift scaffold and facing down his persecutors. We saw an angry lynch mob of Shiites shouting revenge against their onetime Sunni overlord. This was not what the United States was supposed to be fighting for. This was not what our young men and women were dying for. This was not what President Bush had promised a new Iraq would be.

Watching the grainy cell phone images being taped by Maliki's national security adviser, Muaffaq al-Rubai, I was struck that Saddam looked like the most dignified person in the room. He handled the occasion as I expected he would—defiant and unafraid to the end. It was a rushed execution in a dark basement in Baghdad. For me, the final pillar justifying Operation Iraqi Freedom had collapsed. Saddam was not a likable guy. The more you got to know him, the less you liked him. He had committed horrible crimes against humanity. But we had come to Iraq saying that we would make things better. We would bring democracy and the rule of law. No longer would people be awakened by a threatening knock on the door. And here we were, allowing Saddam to be hanged in the middle of the night.

Acknowledgments

Writing this book has been one of the most personally fulfilling experiences of my life. I am thrilled that the day has come when readers can find out for themselves what Saddam Hussein said to the U.S. government when he was in captivity. The minute I met Saddam, I knew that it would result in a book one day. For years, I could speak about my experiences only in a classified setting. However, almost everyone I talked to told me that I should write a book. Unfortunately, by 2011, when it came to finding an agent and a publisher, I was told unequivocally that no one was interested: The American public had moved on and no longer cared about Iraq. Well, the pendulum has swung yet again and Iraq is back on the front pages (I mean that in the digital sense, of course), and suddenly Saddam, and his ouster, seem more relevant than ever. I would like someday to be able to delve more thoroughly into the Ba'athist regime's captured documentation and write a proper and full-blown biography of Saddam.

I began writing this book shortly before I stopped working

for the government in 2011. I continued working on it over weekends in my apartment in Abu Dhabi. I wrote the book mostly because I wanted there to be an accurate record of what Saddam actually said and did not say. So much that had been written about the debriefings was nonsense, by people who were not there or who were there but were not qualified to comment. I realized that this was how the historical record gets filled with nonsense and that if I didn't say my say, well, then I would regret it for the rest of my life.

I would like to thank David Rosenthal, Aileen Boyle, and the team at Blue Rider Press for taking a chance on a first-time author and for their enthusiasm about the book. Working with them has been a wonderful experience.

Most of all I would like to thank my friend Ali Khedery, who helped connect me to my agent, Andrew Wylie. I met Ali during one of my stints in Iraq and enjoyed our many late-night conversations about the mess we were in. Ali is smart, funny, talented, and a kindred spirit on things Iraqi. He is also a patriot who devoted years of his life to help Iraq and America. He needs to write his story.

I could not have published this book without the help and industriousness of my agent, Andrew Wylie, and his staff. Andrew said he would find me a publisher and he did just that. Bravo, Andrew.

I would be remiss if I did not acknowledge the editorial skills of Stephen Smith. Stephen took a rather long and repetitive manuscript and cut it down to most of its present form. He is a gentleman of the old school and I was deeply impressed by, and grateful for, his efforts.

ACKNOWLEDGMENTS

I have profoundly mixed feelings about my thirteen-year career at the CIA. The Agency has such potential (even though it
is well into middle age) and the work it does is so important. It
pains me to see it underperform. I know that I would never have
had many of the experiences I had if I had worked in some other
part of the federal government. And yet, it was so very painful to
see the Agency sink into mediocrity and to deal with managers
who simply did not get why I, and so many others, cared deeply
about what was happening in Iraq. I worked with a number of
analysts who represented some of the best and brightest our
country has to offer. My thanks go to Jamie, Jeff, Chris, Sean,
Mike, Charles, Mike R., Charlie, Jane, Joyce (NTAC), Ami,
Les, Colleen, Mike, Mike B., Ben, Eric, David, Matt, John M.,
Cheryl, Erin, Robert, Doug, Carol, Steve, Vicki, and many others. The American people are well served, and their tax dollars
well spent, by employing such exemplary public servants. I can
actually say about these folks, "Where do we get such people?"
and not mean it sarcastically.

I would like to thank Matt Ross, Jane, Ami, Judith Yaphe,
Deirdre Altman, Cormac Altman, and Ben for taking a look at
the manuscript and offering me their thoughts. Their insights
and criticisms were invaluable; any mistakes or omissions in the
text are mine. Deirdre and Cormac kept prodding me to finish
the book when my work on it had entered a hiatus phase. Lisa
Laforge and her husband, Dave, prodded the text along with
their queries. (Lisa also provided legal advice at a crucial moment. Thanks again.) Matt has often let me use his spacious
Irvine home to write and think about Gulf issues. The pleasure
has been all his!

I would also like to thank David Auslander, Norman Waas, and Mike Perce for their legal advice, as well as one of the more enjoyable dinners in recent memory. Go, Canes!

I would like to thank Dr. Timothy P. Farrell and Dr. Haroon Rashid for their efforts to restore my health during the writing of this book.

I extend my thanks to Dan Hickey, Jim Casey, Margot Morell, and Eli for their help and encouragement in this project. Margot took an afternoon to explain to me over the phone how someone goes about publishing a book, and I greatly appreciate the guidance many years later. Eli, who hails from Lebanon, was a source of information and understanding of the region that ranks up there with scholars at our most prestigious universities. He has enriched my knowledge for many years now.

Family members have been a source of constant support during the writing of this book. Claire, Richard, Nora, and Daniel, as well as their spouses, Jim, Maureen, Tom, and Diana, have always been supportive of my efforts, although they were the first to question my sanity when I told them I was going to Iraq—again! Their children, Joe, Caroline, Ted, Madeline, Paul, and Paige, reinforce my optimism that, regardless of what happens in the world, the future is bright.

Of course, my wife, Barbara, has been my greatest inspiration and my most vocal critic. When she read the book and liked it, I knew it was ready. She has suffered from MS for almost as long as I have known her and yet still keeps an upbeat spirit. If only our government had spent the money designated for invading Iraq on finding cures for diseases or funding a health care system, maybe America would be better off. Just a thought.

I dedicate this book to my mother, Helen, and my father, Richard, who both instilled in me a love for books and, eventually, learning. Without them, my involvement in this story would not have been possible.

About the Author

John Nixon was a senior leadership analyst with the CIA from 1998 to 2011. He did several tours in Iraq and was recognized by a number of federal agencies for his contribution to the war effort. During his time with the CIA, Nixon regularly wrote for, and briefed, the most senior levels of the US government. He also taught leadership analysis to the new generation of analysts coming into the CIA at the Sherman Kent School, the Agency's in-house analytic training centre. Since leaving the Agency in 2011, Nixon has worked as an international risk consultant in Abu Dhabi, UAE. He lives in Alexandria, Virginia. This is his first book.